EFFECTIVE PRAYER

Sergio M. Pineda

BALBOA.
PRESS

A DIVISION OF HAY HOUSE

Balboa Press books may be ordered through booksellers or by contacting:

Balboa Press
A Division of Hay House
1663 Liberty Drive
Bloomington, IN 47403
www.balboapress.com
1 (877) 407-4847

Print information available on the last page.

ISBN: 978-1-9822-0558-4 (sc)
ISBN: 978-1-9822-0560-7 (hc)
ISBN: 978-1-9822-0559-1 (e)

Library of Congress Control Number: 2018906527

Balboa Press rev. date: 06/11/2018

DEDICATED

To all those who suffer in silence. To those who lift their
eyes towards the Heavens with hope. To those who need
an answer. To those who need to touch to believe. To those
who tremble in fear but have never forfeited their courage.

So that the Lord may hear their prayer
and grant them resolution.

CONTENTS

INTRODUCTION

I am not a religious person. I am not even a churchgoer. I am not a pastor, nor do I have a church. But I am very spiritual as a result of philosophical and historical curiosity. I do not take a religious book writing as sacred unless I have personally checked out its historical content against other non-religious sources.

I started a soul-searching project to discover the realm of divinity, a way to find God and a meaning to life that I could comprehend. Since I am quite materialistic, a businessman by nature, I needed to find God's message in a manner in which I could feel and touch. A truth that would give me positive and tangible results. A message that could be developed into a workable formula that can get exact, predictable results every time. For me, the promise of an eternal happy afterlife is of no consequence if I cannot solve first my problems here on this earth.

It has always puzzled me, why so many human beings look at religion as a means of salvation. What are they really looking for? Why do they go to church? Why do they pray so much, but yet, they despise or hurt other people who believe spiritually different.

What I have noticed is that to the great majority of religious persons, their religion does not solve any of their personal problems. In fact the more devoted they are to their beliefs, the more complicated their life becomes.

I want to emphasize that the contents of this book are pragmatic, true and can be put to the test. This information does not intend to preach any religious belief, since it is written from my point of view, which is that of a sinner. As a result, I have no intention of judging any action as good or bad. The information that I provide in this book is a good workable technology for anyone who truly desires to accomplish a dream.

This book is not religious but it does acknowledge a relationship between God as a Creator and his daily relationship with humans, so that they can become creators themselves. In this relationship, I believe that God invites us to create along with Him and offers huge rewards in exchange for our compliance and commitment with this invitation.

This relationship requires following closely a certain protocol. This code of behavior is the Effective way to carry on a prayer'

I admit to writing here what I have interpreted, or translated from many thinkers who had the wisdom to discover the route to happiness and the compassion of having shared their knowledge with the rest of humanity. In sharing this collection of thoughts I am hoping that others can personally benefit by finding the path to their own happiness.

This is a book that synthesizes a universal concept. It is not my intention to offend or criticize any religious philosophy. Simply, I am attempting to explain a practical philosophical reality that affects this physical world, without adhering to any church ideology because **belief in religious dogma is no guarantee of success in life.**

So, I do this, because I see around me a world of individuals that go to mass every Sunday. They celebrate Christmas and Hanukkah and Ramadan, and observe many religious holidays.

They chase eggs during Easter, and they adhere to such customs and fashions because it is the thing to do, without understanding the value of what a relationship with God is meant to be. By missing out on the importance of this simple protocols, they miss out on increasing their own happiness and prosperity.

Follow me and let us explore a bit of the Realm of Divinity by adhering to a process that will take you to a practical relationship with God, in which you will find that life does not need to be a constant struggle, but a path filled with many blessings.

Sergio M. Pineda, 2018

WHY DO WE PRAY?

✠ ✠ ✠

Every one of us prays so that our expectations may come to be realized, or for our suffering to go away. I am not an exception to the daily suffering that affects all of us. It was a few years ago that a personal crisis hit me hard. I saw my older brother slowly wasting away and finally succumbing to cancer. That's when I used to pray like crazy, several times a day, hoping that he would be saved from such a dreaded disease. I became frustrated with my religion when I saw that my prayers, and my family's and even those spoken by my preacher at church went unanswered. *"Prayer is worthless, I thought, it had not produced any desired result for my brother or for myself."* But I was wrong. At the time we just did not know how to pray.

Worse of all, I saw thousands of people praying like crazy every Sunday at church, and then go back home to continue with their same problems and sufferings, with no visible improvement in their lives. Yet, those same people that I saw at church prayed with such devotion and such hope that it motivated me to start exploring the reality of prayer in a more technical manner, and to find its purpose in this life.

Many who do not see the immediate and materialistic result

to prayer, simply ignore any possibility of God's presence even if they claim to be believers.

We pray because we pursue happiness. The only way to achieve happiness is by pleasing the soul. No matter how healthy or rich we may be, if something inside affects our feelings in a negative manner, we will never be happy. We hear constant stories about rich and famous people that were surrounded by every imaginable pleasure, yet they fell into suicidal depressions. Our spiritual side must be attended to and the only way to do this is through effective prayer.

What I have discovered is that lifting my eyes to the heavens and thinking about God or speaking out a request is not a complete prayer. It is only a temporary invocation, and therefore it is not enough. A casual introverted muttering such as "Lord help me" may or may not be heard by God. In fact, I believe that silent prayers can NOT be heard by God. Neither is believing the new age mantra that everything is all about "positive attitude".

"Both optimists and pessimists contribute…
The optimist invents the aeroplane,
the pessimist the parachute". - George B. Shaw

The positive and negative thinkers, each has their valid points of view and each has a different expectation of what a good answer from God will be. I believe that God gave us freedom of thought so that we could explore all our options – good and bad – before expressing them out loud. He cannot hear your proper presentation unless you express it out loud and with an implemented plan.

Praying for myself

I must say here that Prayer is effective when the person prays for himself or herself. Not so effective when he prays for others.

The reason is because when a person prays he demonstrates a willingness to change.

This book is for the person that wants to improve his or her life by getting God to respond. What this person needs to realize first, is that life is a series of moments lived in cycles and that we usually carry out these cycles mostly by habit and not very well thought out. These cycles which are sometimes described as laws of eventuality", where a person that smokes cigarettes or eats excessively eventually finds himself or herself sick, are actions that are never projected into the future and yet they are the cause of ailments that we then try to correct with prayer.

Because prayer is a specific request, before requesting anything from someone, wouldn't I have to answer some questions about myself and about my capabilities?

I can't simply ask for a car without knowing beforehand how I would drive it, maintain it, how I would use it, where would I go with it and whether my eyesight was good enough.

Certainly, I would have to have some knowledge about the person I am addressing my request to, and what this request is all about. More importantly, what purpose will this request serve?

We pray because we want something. The chances of success in finding something or someone are based on a process. To search in a disorganized manner, without knowing the terrain and without the appropriate tools, is to search in vain. Your chances are the same as winning the lottery without buying a ticket.

To pray is to look for answers from God and finding God is fortunately a relatively easy thing to do. But to be successful in our prayer we must be in condition to pray, in the same way that a football player must be in a good physical condition to play.

Knowing all these things and addressing them to God, in a proper way, is a prayer.

Doing it within a process makes it an effective prayer.

The things you hide in your heart…
Eat you alive! – unknown

What do people really pray about? Generally, we ask God's favor for help in satisfying one of the pleasures of life, or in turning things around so that we may once again enjoy the pleasures of life. Basically, we ask for the removal of pain. No one really likes the pain that comes about as we lose our pleasures. But in a world that has two opposing sides to everything, where a person treads in the balance between good and bad, between light and dark, it is easy to tumble and fall out of grace into the opposite side of pleasure.

Praying for others:

"If you are not making someone else's life better,
then you are wasting your time. Your life will become better
by making other people's lives better" – Will Smith

The person praying for others is hoping that the other person will change, and that is a different story because God may not interfere with the other person's free will.

However, granting LOVE to others is the faster and more effective manner of praying for someone else.

I have always been bothered that at the sign of a tragedy many people will send thoughts and prayers as though this was an effective way to help the victims.

Instead what I learned is that, if the person sends Love, in a manner that satisfies one of life's pleasures, to the victim(s), this recipient does get relief. And relief, even if only temporary, is a blessing. Sending thought and prayers is an empty effort unless you are willing to offer some alleviation to the anguish of the victim.

How is this love expressed? Simple, by granting a bit of one or more of the following pleasures:

1. *FOOD and TASTE*
       "My wife is upset with me…but still made me great supper"
2. *RESTFUL SLEEP*
       "He worked until late… next morning keep quiet"
3. *COMFORT AND SECURITY*
       "Your bills are paid…I got some groceries for you"
4. *AROMATIC SCENT*
       "Let's go for a walk through the garden"
5. *MUSIC AND RHYTHMIC WORDS.*
       "Would you like me to read you some poetry or play your favorite record?"
6. *TOUCH AND SEX*
       "Cuddling time"
7. *WELLNESS*
       "How about a walk this morning?"
8. *COMPANIONSHIP*
       "I am visiting mom this afternoon"
9. *KNOWLEDGE*
       "I will get you the information on that tax issue
10. *BEAUTY & ORDER*
       "Macy's is having a sale on your favorite _____ today?
       "Let's paint that outside porch"
11. *INSPIRATION*
       "How about a visit to the museum today?"
12. *ECSTASY*
       "Thank you, I really needed that!"
13. *PEACE / SERENITY*
       "When was the last time you looked up at the stars and saw the Milky Way?

14. *PURPOSE*
    "You are excellent at _____"
15. *RECOGNITION*
    "I really admire you for _____"
16. *PARENTHOOD*
    "What a beautiful bundle of joy"

When you do this for others, you remove for that moment any feeling of stress and depression. There is no greater pleasure than receiving one of these favors and especially when you receive them on a daily basis from someone who shows *Care.*

We do not categorize our prayers, but in general we address a topic that is related to the opposite of these pleasures.

"You feel so lost, so cut off, so alone. Only you are not.
See, in all our searching, the only thing we've found
That makes the emptiness bearable, is each other" – Carl Sagan

No person likes Hunger, Stress, Abandonment, Rottenness, Noise, Loneliness, Sickness, Ignorance, Ugliness, Depression, Pain, Despair, Poverty, Indifference, Insignificance and Sterility and yet all are the darker sides of life we ask God for help in removing.

Acts of love such as acts of mercy, acts of charity, acts of compromise, acts of patience, acts of forgiveness and acts of giving are all actions of EFFECTIVE praying for someone else.

I personally experienced the pain of living with a person that had an addiction. I loved this person immensely and tried all forms of helping and praying for him. I prayed for years and nothing happened to change his condition. It was a case of praying like crazy and nothing happened. The harder I tried the angrier he got. But in time, what I grew to realize is that prayer changed ME. And I started to accept the fact that if I loved him that much, then

I had to live and accept his condition. And the only way I could help was by granting him Love whenever it was possible. Giving a bit of one of these pleasures EVERYDAY if he was accessible, in temper or physical condition, to receive it. So I satisfied, or tried my best to satisfy a bit of those pleasures I describe above. Many would call it enabling, and many including the addict would say that his condition was my fault; but in granting acts of love and giving I discovered peace for both of us because the addict simply seeks and believes what his own subconscious mind tells him is necessary for his survival. So by praying for him in this manner the relationship works despite the sorrow of seeing the addict slowly waste away.

Ever wonder why hard liquors are called Spirits? The answer may be thousands of years old when the Arabs called the drinks Al-ghawl or Al-ghoul by Europeans, and referred in the Koran (verse 37:47) to a drink of bad effect, demonic or evil result.

Even then, Muslim mankind knew that these drinks summoned and then released spirits or ghouls of evil onto the human soul. Christianity in America pushed for Prohibition for the same reason. In fact, The United States is so tormented by alcohol that it is the only country that has two constitutional amendments regarding alcohol. One that prohibits and one that allows it. In time, we discovered that these spirits can be released by many other substances and that a simple governmental law mandating them illegal is no deterrent against the Devil's effort to control a person.

However, we have come to scientifically realize that most of our personal problems arise as a result of living in a society where issues that cause pain and anxiety are related to bad drinking, poor diets or addictive behavior. These prevent the person from acquiring the necessary knowledge or wisdom to see clearly through his/her problems.

But personal and effective prayer is the answer to displace the devils influence and limit his access to the human body. In fact, only by turning to God in effective prayer, one can rid him or herself of addiction. It is the ONLY way. Do not waste time in psychiatry or medication for they are only temporary solutions. Any AA member will tell you this!

Evil is a real force that dwells inside the human spirit to prevent us from enjoying the pleasures that God wants to give us. At some early point in our lives that evil entered in some form of trauma and started to control our subconscious thought process. For many years that evil prevents us from doing any self soul search or pursuit of wisdom. Evil will trade you a single moment of overindulgence for a lifetime of pain. If you do not believe this look at a person that got drunk one night but is now in jail (or in pain) for life. The reason for his jail time is not important. The question should be: why was evil in control?

Evil is not threatened by intelligence but it is very afraid of wisdom. Therefore, it is a force that can be displaced by prayer.

To help the wounded loved one, you must take his hand –physically take his hand – and pray with that person. In that prayer session ask the questions that trouble his/her mind and then find what pleasure you can provide.

People in pain have trouble releasing the information that is needed to affect a positive change because evil does not want to identify itself. To help that person, prayer is effective when there is a one to one connection. The prayer for another in which you hold his hand is to obtain information and understanding. Do not attempt to give advice or be judgmental when a person starts to release his deepest thoughts.

I experienced the sad passing of my brother from bone cancer. Throughout the long and painful ordeal I prayed for him to be cured. But what I failed to realize was that he was not praying for the same things I was praying for. In both the addict and the infirm I was praying for what I BELIEVED they should be doing or should happen to them, as though I wanted to control the situation. It was my prayer, according to MY judgement. But not theirs. Inside their minds and their hearts they had different desires and different opinions of how they wanted their condition to develop - or not develop. For them it was a "thanks, but no thanks" situation where they accepted my prayer (but dismissed my effort and advise) because they had plans of their own for dealing with their issues.

You can change yourself, but you can't change anyone else unless THEY make the determination to change. That person needs to find through HIS own prayer what is their new reality for survival and happiness. Sometimes when YOU change yourself, others will be encouraged to change by seeing your efforts, determination and success.

You may inspire them and that inspiration will be an answer to YOUR prayers for them.

You can pray for others that an ailment may go away but that prayer will not be answered until the person with the sickness is determined to confront the root of the problem along with all its associations. That change, with the time and commitment required to obtain the cure, is the difficulty. Anyone who has tried changing any habit, a diet, an exercise program, an image of themselves realizes how difficult it is. But in the meantime, understand that life is a series of moments and that in each of those moments you have the ability to grant a bit of pleasure to your loved one, to help him or her deal with their struggle. God rewards your giving and also extends the life of the loved one.

The purpose of effective prayer is to focus on pleasures and pray to obtain and maintain them. We seek these pleasures because they are the natural antidotes to depression, anxiety, anger, hatred, ignorance and a series of other causes of pain.

It is easier to ask for God's grace and help when you are blessed that to ask for His favor once you have fallen into the darkness and you seek salvation from the antithesis of pleasure. After all, when you are granted any of the pleasures you are receiving a blessing, and when you don't have them, you hurt.

Because our existence is based on the concept of duality, where we need others to give and receive, our prayers will be cause and consequence of our pursuit of these pleasures and it is important to avoid mistakes of overindulgence in these pleasures that would only flip us over to the painful side.

Granting a bit of pleasure does not mean "giving YOURSELF away to others", or giving yourself away to debauchery. It means gifting what is reasonable to demonstrate that you care, and to benefit ourselves and others we must exercise effort, organization and control.

This formula of granting LOVE is the message of Christ. Feed the hungry….Clothe the poor…hug the crying…educate the innocent etc. These are the acts that benefit the victim. This is the way to pray for them.

When you pray with someone grant him or her a gift of Love. Make an offering to someone else. In a Catholic service, the church demonstrates this act of love by requesting that you look around to fellow churchgoers and offer serenity ("may peace be with you") and the Priest offers bread and wine. This representation of the body and the blood of Christ is a way to show that Jesus loved his disciples so much that in an act of Love, He willingly offered his own flesh and blood to feed mankind.

Communion is an act of love. Communion is meant to represent every one of the above described pleasures.

You do not need to be at church to make this offering. If by granting these pleasures as a favor to your loved one (s), even in small amounts on a daily basis, and if your partner gives them back in return, you will be in communion and your relationship with that person will last forever in happiness.

Therefore, the continuation of this book is about making prayer effective for the person who is praying. Not for others. Once he/she find that prayer has resulted in desired results then, and only then, the blessed person can proceed in the difficult path of educating others, even children, in how to pray to receive blessings. In the meantime, only acts of love can bring relief, if at least momentarily, to others.

2

WHO DO WE PRAY TO?

✠ ✠ ✠

It has always puzzled me, why so many human beings look at religion as a means of personal peace and salvation. What are they really looking for? Why do they attend a church? Why they send thoughts and prayers, but yet, they despise or hurt others who believe spiritually differently.

Worse of all, I see hundreds of people that pray like crazy and then go back to continue with their same problems and sufferings with no visible improvements in their lives. Many who do not see the immediate and materialistic result to prayer, simply ignore any possibility of God's presence even if they claim to be believers.

Where then is God?

I don't think there is a person that can ascertain with precision when the concept of God first appeared.

Thousands of years ago, as the first humans developed a consciousness they must have seen their surroundings and felt that they were not alone.

It is impossible to assume that it was a feeling of impotence when confronted with the vastness of nature and the infinity of the skies. Humans are by nature arrogant and feel supreme over any other species.

So, the presence of God must have manifested itself in a deep rooted connection of all living things.

There is an instinct for survival in all living forms that not only forces us to become creative but also makes us question our origin and purpose in this world. It is an instinct that brings out fear whenever we feel threatened, anxiety or insecurity about our condition. When we seek the help or advice of other people we discover that such feeling of worry is also present in others.

However, in that connection between all of us, we feel the presence of an Energy that not only binds us but it is the only possible invisible physical force that can resolve our most pressing problems.

Some people, dismiss this force as only a superstition and others have assigned supernatural names to identify it.

The problem of humanity has been that MOST of us Do feel the presence of that Energy but have had a big problem with its identity, its location and its reach.

The people that dismiss this Energy are the Atheists that either cannot accept what they cannot see or are afraid that such Energy will not resolve any human issues.

We all call this Energy God and we either accept it or dismiss it.

The atheist has given up on seeking the aid of a higher power because he will not believe in what he cannot see. Atheism therefore, is a religion in itself and the Atheist believes in his/her atheism with the same passion as the religious believer.

Yet for the believer the question persists: "If I have faith and there is a God, can I get help from God to ease the struggles of life?

Both Atheist and believer cannot escape suffering nor anxiety. Both seek the same pleasures.

So this book is for the believer who seeks answers from God.

The person looking for a common ground where the existence of God must be proved to justify their purpose in this life.

By ignoring or denying the presence of God the atheist puts aside any conflict between his soul and the real world he lives in. He simply believes in mind and body and behaves and thinks like any other living species in the planet that grudgingly accepts the impositions of life on him. Life happens, its temporary, and ends.

The believer instead, looks for his inner soul and a connection to a supreme force that hopefully will help to ease the struggle that the real world imposes on him. To him life is a gift, it's eternal and never ends, and God is a necessity as a guide for all important decisions and a protector from bad situations throughout the path of life.

The atheist looks for pragmatism and science as a way to ease these burdens of life whereas the believer latches on to hope because that is the last sentiment to be lost.

Although the atheist is right in his practical approach to life, he is wrong in his denial of God and whereas the believer may be wrong in his approach to faith, he is right in feeling the presence of God.

But how can a person prove this presence of God?

We can prove the existence of God by asking for his grace and receiving it.

I will tell you how I found it. I started my search like a beachcomber that periodically finds and collects valuable items along the way, and started to compile a set of concepts that are not necessarily religious but are found in the Bible as well as in most religious books. I found these concepts to be totally true and they can be placed to the test.

The search of the atheist for his personal problems is always through scientific approach but his denial of any spirituality may take away his internal peace.

The believer has the advantage of not only enjoying the results of science but of obtaining the aid of God if he can understand that **science is proof of God's existence**. But if the believer chooses to deny science, he will then be actually worse off than the atheist who in turn, at least, has a pragmatic path to progress.

> *Everything we call real is made of things*
> *that can not be regarded as real, if quantum*
> *mechanics hasn't profoundly shocked you,*
> *you haven't understood it yet". - Niels Bohr*

Both, religious and scientific writings admit to a universe created by an energy event that scattered millions of particles. At the time religious books were written, the science was not there to understand the concept of the Big Bang.

However, even back then, humans understood that we are nothing more than particles of dust in in an incredible large space. This, being a scientific reality tells us that the best search for God is in quantum physics.

Quantum is the study of super tiny particles including atoms. So tiny are all of these particles that they cannot be seen by the human eye. Some of these particles are so super small that they can only be found by mathematical deduction.

Up until approximately 70 years ago, not many believed that in front of their own eyes and noses, billions of particles called atoms filled and surrounded the very transparent air they breathed. Worse of all, they would not believe that these invisible atoms were shaped like tiny solid solar systems themselves.

Not many believed until clever scientists took it upon to separate one of these atoms and then implode it. The result was the Atomic bomb and the total destruction of Hiroshima and

Nagasaki. Denial had met the face of destruction and fear made invisible science supreme.

This event was new and unique. Before, silent and unseen death had come in manners that humans believed were punishments from God. But this time it was a human creation. Just as invisible and deadly.

Although invisible, we all now believe in atoms and in their incredible power, and three realities came forth after this atomic result:

First, there is great energy within a quantum particle.

Second, **Someone** can exert control over this particle.

Third, the quantum particle cannot see the controller but it's subject to his power.

If you have ever seen a picture of the galaxies then it is easy to understand that we humans are quantum particles.

We humans are quantum particles made of even smaller quantum particles. That is how small we are, yet we have been made with the same properties of the star dust that permeates the universe.

We have free will to move and act in all sorts of manner and direction.

And, we can also be directed by that **Someone** that can exert control.

In the bigger laboratory we call the universe, **Someone** is God.

It is not important what you think of God. You can choose your own concept of God if this makes it easier to understand His presence and His participation in your creation.

From the moment that the big bang happened God spread the seed of consciousness to every corner of the universe. This seed had intent of life and created matter space and time. At this point your conscious soul was created and you started your own creation.

Each one created the world in which it could attain a material form and developed itself onto whichever entity was the easiest.

"Looking for consciousness in the brain,
Is like looking inside the radio for the
announcer" - Nassim Haramein

At all times this consciousness has been one united source like a lake that constantly spills over creating millions of creeks that run in different directions. Billions of individual entities formed and had a cycle of birth, life, death and reincarnation. No part of this consciousness would be ever wasted or destroyed. The so called death would be the fertile soil of the upcoming birth.

The consciousness of the prey would be absorbed by its predator and the predator become subject to the spirit of its prey. Consciousness was the energy of life and as time passed it grew in sophistication until it became self-aware. It was the rise of man.

Ever since, man has understood that no soul ever dies but it becomes something else at the discretion of God. But every man or woman or living thing does not have the same attention from God. Just like in the laboratory where a scientist will pay more attention to the particles that act according to his purpose, God in bigger scales is always watching over those that are reacting positively to Him.

Since the beginning all life forms understand that they will become predator and prey but that they are accountable for each life or energy they take. The taking with waste or for self-indulging will be penalized. In the next cycle of rebirth the penalty shall be to have a lower life form than the present. Just like a parent gifts the best items to the caring son but penalizes the wasteful son by giving him lesser worth. They both receive because they are both loved. But to he who best cares, the best is given. If you were to give away two cars, wouldn't you give your best car to the son that will best take care of it?

Places like India honor their cows for that reason. In the Amazon some tribes honor monkeys and other animals in similar fashion. Buddhist in Tibet will not even kill an insect so as to not injure a life form that could eventually cause a bad karma. They believe in "Don't kill the insects so that you may not become an insect in your next life."

God, the universal soul

The universe is God's self
A part of him - these creatures all!
In him their birth, they live in him,
and into him they end withal!
The mortal ever toils and works,
and as he sows upon this earth,
in virtue's soil or ways of sin,
so he reaps in a future birth!-
(The Upanishads - Hidden Wisdom - Aprox. 1000 B.C.)

Ever since man became self-aware he has understood that he carries a soul or spirit that controls his mind and his body. But unlike other animals, he searches for the owner of that soul. For the source to which he returns. This is the search for God.

The search for God is not in the stars. It is not in religion. It is in this self-awareness.

How do we call God?

I used to attend church in the hopes of gaining some practical technology to access and work with God. After all, I took time to go to school to learn design, and I went to piloting school to learn how to fly. In those schools, I received the technology that I was expecting.

Whereas in every flying school they teach the same process, in church it is different. The different churches have been greatly responsible for creating confusion about accessing God. The confusion arises because each preacher is a director that shows us a different view. This confusion, sometimes creates either religious fanatics or, in my case, a bored churchgoer who attends on Sunday just to comply with a family expectation. In all my life I never learned at church a system to access God. I never learned what the process of prayer was all about.

I know that if I want to call someone who lives across town, I need a telephone, and I also need the person's telephone number, and finally I need to figure out how to use the phone. These three things must be done properly and in a prearranged order so that the other party can answer the call. Common sense would tell me that I also need a process to call God.

So, prayer is simply a call to God seeking His help in order to create cycles that make us happier. With the same idea that you would search for instructions to fly an airplane, calling on God requires this learning. Do so because you want to create an effective relationship with God that will bring you the much needed pleasures associated with love, health, wisdom and prosperity.

God does not set harsh terms on those seeking Him. He is concerned with us when we want Him enough. You are a particle that wants to call His attention. Therefore, do the things that cause Him to get interested and involved in your life. God is interested in the loyalty you show Him in your consciousness, because this determines who you really are.

Before talking about God and our relationship with Him, it is important to talk about us humans and our relationship between us. After all, the relationship that we develop with God is nothing more than the reflection of our relationship with other humans.

Assuming that God was not the most important thing in your life, or that He had no effect on our lives, we would still have to deal with the reality that other humans do affect our life.

A prayer is not only a conversation with God. It is an action to communicate with God so that He can make our relationship with other humans improve in such a way that those other humans can help us. It is worthless to pray to God and ignore your neighbor.

In our call to God, you are the telephone, Wisdom secrets are the number, and you need to dial by way of a Divine Cycle.

Calling God requires a bit of learning time. You have to learn a bit about the use of the "telephone". Yes –YOU. Unfortunately, a lot of people find themselves too busy or too arrogant to dedicate themselves to look inward and discover themselves.

Discovering yourself is an essential part of the process. You might discover items and issues that are blocking or damaging the "telephone" and that need acceptance and repair.

Praying without learning to apply wisdom to the Cycle process is not effective.

Going back to our analogy with the telephone call to God, the human spirit is the telephone, and unfortunately we may know a lot about our surroundings but for some reason we hate to look inwards and realize our total capabilities. So we learn a lot of things, about other things, except about ourselves. We are busy in many things, except to take care of our bodies and our spirit. We are the telephone set, but do not know how to manage our own physical and mental equipment. In millions of cases a person will succeed in business, only to die young from a disease caused by overweight or excessive smoking. This was partly the case of my own brother. He would take care of everyone and everything, except of his own person.

*"If the brain is the radio's receiver, then the Heart
is the dial tuning the radio to the frequency
of your choice"* - Nassim Haramein

However, the spirit is a powerful transmitter, and everything in the universe is simply a manifestation of the spirit. So essentially we can accomplish any task we set out to do if we follow a process. No task is too difficult if you design your process right. So make your call to God and follow your process. This process will be YOUR Divine Cycle of Prayer.

3

THE DIVINE CYCLE

✠ ✠ ✠

Making prayer work through a cycle

It is important to realize what the process of prayer is all about. The process of prayer is a cycle. One by which you find yourself first, then you find God, and then you learn to carry a continuous relationship with Him that benefits you.

Since I am looking for God in a very real, tangible and practical manner, I looked for the first step of the process in the laws of physics. There, I found that all scientific theories could be summarized in the following rule: The creation of the entire universe, including the conduct of all living and passive matter, is a reflection on the way God thinks.

God thinks that everything should follow a certain order. A process if you will. That all things that come to be realized are first conceived in thought, spoken, then acted upon, then worked through and completed to their death. And death becomes an understructure for what is to be reborn.

It took God seven steps to complete the creation of our Universe. The Bible describes it as seven days, but a day to God could be a billion years to me. Einstein explained that time is relative to the decay of different forms of matter. So, in reality, time is only important because we want to measure how long it takes for something to happen before our bodies decay in this life. For this reason, I do not pay much attention to the description of time in religious books.

But I do pay attention to processes in religious books because Order is pleasure and it brings about good things. As described in the Bible, the first step of Creation was the Big Bang. In this first step where He said: *Let there be light*!, and God created only energy. Perhaps He could have created everything with the big bang. From the galaxies to the humans with a big instant POW! But He didn't because in doing so, that would have been like an instantaneous camera flash that would only capture and freeze His creation. Instead, He did it step by step. He placed in perfect order each thing carefully after the previous step was completed to His satisfaction. It was a perfect sequence. Each thing placed would have a perfect cycle of start, action, and duration so that the cycle of creation could keep on going, like a giant wheel, for all eternity. **This is the Divine Cycle. This is the eternity of God.**

God's creation was simple. First he created a three-dimensional space in which he placed two elements to toy with. These two elements are Matter and Energy. The alteration of these two elements would affect everything, including us. Such alteration would be made in a cycle and create a new cycle itself. In this manner God's creation and His eternity would have to be respected.

This universal cycle is one of thought, words, action (work), and resurrection. This is a cycle applicable to all things in biology and physics. It manifests itself with all material things and immaterial situations, in our personal relationships, in our goals and in every aspect of our life.

Therefore, a personal problem could actually be tackled by establishing a cycle similar to any of the many processes that you may follow at your daily workplace. By comparatively visualizing a process, within a topic that you may know perfectly well, the solution will materialize. This is the reason that Jesus spoke in parables. He would tell a story that could be visualized, and which was applicable to the resolution of many situations.

An engineer, for example, could solve a problem that he may have with his son, using the same reasoning that he would use in designing and building a bridge. This is possible because, changing matter and energy through a cycle that he knows, created both his son and the bridge.

In my daily business as a building designer and Real Estate Developer, I see a project born from the moment the investor thinks of an idea. His thought process requires a great deal of mental energy. Then, he will make presentations to partners, banks and other government entities. By doing this, his thought has been put into words. His words are acted upon and soon other people are also working the project. The project will have a limited useful life and will then be demolished. But it is demolished to give way to a new idea or design and the space will then be used for a new project.

The cycle can be summarized in

THOUGHT, WORD, ACTION, and RE-START.

I omit the word death because in every situation, death is only a completed stage that requires a new start.

Thought
Re-Start

Actions
(Work)   Word

The Cycle is the process of any creation, a creation by your action or by your omission. The cycle can be used for a good or a bad creation.

To create is not the same as to invent. An inventor designs a new product, whereas creation is the ability to organize existing resources and events to make a new or ageless concept or item work.

We spend our lives moving in cycles. From the time the alarm clock wakes us up, our minds are full of thoughts, some very simple, others more complicated, but all of them start a cycle. My Mother wakes up with the thought of preparing the morning breakfast, describes it to my Dad and proceeds to follow the cycle to completion.

But not all cycles are this habitual. Some are very complex and we step into them without sufficient knowledge and we try to wade through them as best we can, but unfortunately we end up with terrible results. These are cycles of which we have little or no control over. We call them problems.

But problems dissolve when we regain a measure of control over them.

The way to regain control over a rickety cycle is to ask God to bless it, and to seek order in that aspect of your life again.

The cycle becomes Divine ONLY when accompanied by prayer.

Through prayer, you guide the Cycle with God's intervention. You will know when to act and when to omit. You will be in control, because God will always be there, as your partner, in obtaining your objective.

Humans already have all the necessary elements in this universe to achieve their creations. They just have to go through the proper cycles. When the cycles are well-executed humanity progresses. When our leaders fail, they do so because they create destructive cycles, and war and discord arise.

God wants us to execute them well. Every time that God has placed someone to a test it has been with the intention of showing the effect of a well-executed Divine Cycle. The life of Jesus is a perfectly executed cycle. Jesus was conceived from Divine thought, grew to explain the word, acted courageously with faith to demonstrate the power of prayer, worked with an organization of apostles to spread the message and finally died as a human to demonstrate the resurrection and eternity of the spirit.

On a more palpable note we can say that the success of America as a nation has been the ability of our Founding Fathers to take the thoughts of democracy and write them down as a constitution, where its words are still valid almost three centuries later. Then, acting, first against the British and thereafter, against all enemies to defend those words and before long working the land with all its resources to build a great nation.

God is interested in guiding us through a good cycle, and that good guidance is obtained through prayer.

At the same time, God allows us a free will. For millions of years, The Earth was ruled by life forms that conformed to the law of a perfect but unregulated cycle of creation. Those life forms that could not organize themselves effectively died out. It was truly a survival of the fittest where sentiment and empathy did not exist. Or at least, these feelings did not matter. Then in the last step of the creation cycle, the human factor was introduced, and with it came all those virtues that converted the simplicity of Creation, into the most complex game.

Now, with humans in the scene, sentiment affected thought in a multitude of ways. Free choice allowed us to start cycles that were more ambitious than the simple survival cycles that ruled the animal kingdom. A different sentiment about the same item could trigger cycles that would have totally different results. Whereas, all lions must follow the predetermined order of always being the hunter to live, each human could have thousands of lifestyle options. Each member of the human race can actually behave like a different species, with each mind having a unique vision of the universe. God really meant it when he said we could have free will.

Now the cycle of creation, which for millions of years seemed perfectly organized albeit a bit boring, entered a period of true vivacity. A wild ride in which, like a bunch of rowdy drunkards, humans have approached the brink of total destruction.

An effective prayer is a completion of a Divine cycle.

"Here is the prime condition of success: Concentrate your energy, thought and capital exclusively upon the business in which you are engaged." - Andrew Carnegie

Think it, voice it, work it! It's that easy. Only by expressing your desires to God in orderly manner, can He intervene. It is like inviting someone into a deal. Once they accept they will most likely enjoy participating in your event. Therefore, think out your petition, express it in words, first to God, then to others, and take action to make it happen. Then work through it until completion.

After you are done with the first stage – repeat it by kicking it up a notch. Polish your thoughts, prepare a better presentation, time your actions, work different angles and finish by thinking out your next stage.

You can accomplish anything by following and completing Divine cycles. At first your cycles may be simple and their completion is fast. But as your communication with God improves and your purposes grow, they will become spirals by which your wisdom and prosperity will increase exponentially.

Be aware of the fact that a thought, ANY thought, can commence a cycle. Those Cycles without prayer get started and completed sometimes without control. Let's say that a cycle was started from anger. You thought someone had tried to hurt you or that you received a lousy service. So your first thought was to "*kick that person's butt*". You then didn't measure your words and your temper flared in a way that your actions became abusive or aggressive towards someone else. This is a cycle that has placed you in a position of destruction without you having the time to realize it. By omission and carelessness many people have managed to create downward spirals that end in disaster.

Thoughts of anger, thoughts of hatred, thoughts of vengeance are all thoughts that can start destructive cycles that can be guided not by God, but by evil forces. Words of anger, words of hatred, words of retribution are the arrows of the devil. Be very careful that you may not become an accomplice to evil because your acts will take you into a cycle to your own ruin.

4

SEEKING WISDOM

✠ ✠ ✠

Wisdom is the way in which a person or a group of individuals have learned to search for God, and to establish a beneficial relationship with their spirit. It is the ability to learn and enjoy the subjective things in life such as beauty, sentiment, perception, virtues, pleasures, morals, and many other unseen realities that define our relationship as spiritual beings and that produce benefits in our prosperity.

Wisdom is not the same as intelligence. Many intelligent people are despots or criminals. Jails are full of intelligent people. These people are not wise. And without wisdom, prosperity does not stay with the crooks permanently, and inevitably their purposes eventually also crumble.

"One way to define wisdom is the ability to see,
into the future, the consequences of your
choices in the present." - Andy Andrews

We live to acquire knowledge and work this knowledge. If the process to achieve wisdom of an individual or group is true, then such knowledge should bring that person(s) continuous prosperity and increased happiness.

There are two ways to acquire wisdom, the first is by **study and application** and the second is by **the impact of getting knocked down by life.** Both methods provide experience.

"Teachers will open the door,
but you must enter by yourself" – Zen Proverb

By study, we attempt to understand the purpose and feelings of someone else's previous project. We try to garnish as much experience as possible so that we may not commit or repeat mistakes. Unfortunately, the process of study is repetitive and not very exciting and the lack of energetic action prompts many to discard it at an early age. This is sad because as boring as study may be it is at least quite safe.

Mistakes, on the other hand, teach us through the hard knocks or impacts of life. Mistakes are painful, expensive and they are the result of not acquiring the right technology during study. Incredibly though, it is the most common system of learning used by humanity. People go through great efforts and pains, sacrificing time, health and possessions, to achieve short moments of pleasure.

Sometimes people say: *"what was he thinking?"* when a person destroys his life over a moment he thought was going to be pleasurable.

But people do destroy valuable things, that took great effort to build up, in minutes. And their experience is only valuable AFTER their cycle of destruction is over. The impact that life produces stays with them forever like an awful scar.

"Experience is the teacher of all things" – Julius Caesar

Impact is the chosen system of the mentally lazy and is what we can expect when we enter the playing field without knowledge or proper coaching. Those who learn by impact have a life that is a constant battle. Much like a gladiator's existence, entering into fights and maturing by painful experience until they finally succumb without really having prospered or enjoyed happiness.

We have the opportunity to find wisdom and we have these two avenues, of which the easiest is by study. So take a little more than an hour on Sunday; Take the whole day, and get your life back.

Wisdom defines and corrects your process of thought. Seek wisdom and you will find God. This is the first step of the cycle.

WISDOM IS THE ONLY ROAD TO THE FAVORS OF GOD.

"My life – my personality, my habits, even my speech – is a combination of the books I choose to read, the people I choose to listen to, and the thoughts I choose to tolerate in my mind" – Andy Andrews

When God appeared to King Solomon and offered him anything, the king chose wisdom because by having wisdom he could have everything. There is a Divine mandate that states:

The greater your knowledge of God, the greater your prosperity.

We must seek wisdom because the answers we seek are not given to us automatically. If everything in our lives were left up to God's will, then why get out of bed and make any effort? After all, everything would already be pre-determined and any action would just be a waste of time.

When faced with a personal struggle, the person must therefore ask internal questions about himself that require changes in thought, attitude and behavior. To receive these answers, he must meditate.

"To the mind that is still,
the whole universe surrenders" – Lao Tzu

Meditation brings you to wisdom and Wisdom gives you the answers to live better. Once you have these answers, which usually call for changes in your life, the next step is to seek God's help through prayer. This is actually the reason why wise men took the very long time, and extreme effort to write what we now call our holy books. The authors were interested in our survival growing up in a hostile environment.

RELIGION IS NOT A PATH TO FIND GOD.

Initially, as a religious person, I used to attend church in the hopes of gaining some practical knowledge to access and work with God. Like most, I simply listened to the church's dogma. After all, as a professional I took time to go to school and listen to teachers to learn about my career and I received the technology that I was expecting.

But the simple act of attending church is not sufficient. Whereas in every business school they teach a similar process, in church it is different. The different churches have been greatly responsible for creating confusion about accessing God. The confusion arises because each preacher is a director that shows us a different cut of the movie. Some versions are excellent but a lot of them are crummy. This confusion, sometimes creates either religious fanatics or, in my case, an eventually bored catholic churchgoer who attended on Sunday just to comply with a family expectation. In all my life I never learned through a church a system to access God.

I was born a catholic. Like most people religious faith is something that my parents chose for me and most likely the faith that their parents chose for them. And it's been like that for generations before me.

*"To the believer, only his religion is perfect….
all others are imperfect" - SMP*

That is the world we live in. One in which we believe in what our parents told us to believe in. We never questioned the cultural or religious beliefs in which we grew. If we questioned we were, and still are heavily berated or even punished. The set of beliefs is supposed to be sacred, respected above any other thoughts or beliefs.

So many of us are very fond of our religious heritage and upbringing. Yet we know very little about our own religion. For this reason, a preacher, pastor or Imam can sway or modify a person's personality and introduce not only issues of faith but also factors of fashion, conduct, and even hate.

A Christian reading the Old Testament – Book of Leviticus - for the first time may be shocked to read his or her tattoos, diets of lobster, shrimp and pork, and other modern behaviors are sinful. Or the Muslim, who thinks he/she is certain regarding what is halal (appropriate) and Haram (prohibited) by religious law. These same believers consider themselves a good religious person for simply believing the words of their church.

At the risk of sounding offensive, I can assert that every person that thinks they are religious are simply following a human opinion. That is what a church is: A human opinion on how YOU should live your life within the society that surrounds you. And that is why there are so many of them.

It is also the reason why humans walk around in confusion without being able to comprehend what is happening in their daily lives. Some blame the bad weather or natural disasters on the sinful behavior of others. Others thank God for things that God had nothing to do with.

But all of them would like to call on God when a need arises and all of them would like to get a response.

Religion will not give you access to God and being religious won't get you the answers you need. I know this sounds awfully sinister, but the reality is that segregating your thoughts into what a religious dogma teaches, will only separate you from the favor of God.

The constant quarrel over the veracity of religious belief has left many questioning whether God is the creator of man or whether man created this imaginary friend and called Him God.

True, history tells us the many times in which mankind would build an effigy out of stone or precious metal and then admire the sculpture and called it a God.

At first an act of good luck would make it seem as though the effigy had power and it was adored and prayers made to it. In time, when no other good results came from it was changed or destroyed…and God and His existence questioned.

Humans want a God they can see and touch and connect with in a very materialistic manner and grow frustrated when they cannot find Him.

Yet, they can't seem to be able to simply deny Him. At some point of human history, the most powerful and influential of kings must have looked at the skies and his natural surroundings and asked himself if there was a being more powerful than him. After all, if a king was a supreme being amongst his own people and could control their life and property rights, who then, controlled the effects of nature such as floods and earthquakes and thunder and rain that were out of the control of the most powerful kings?

The natural assumption was that there must be a God or Gods. The Greeks came forth with a variety of Gods and their centaurs and minotaurs. Each God was shown in the sky when human ignorance could not yet discern the planets.

Then, we hear of the golden cow built by pagan Jews after their exodus from Egypt. The God Baal represented as a furious bull. The ancient Egyptian Gods represented as hawks and foxes. The ancient American cultures making totem poles representing bears and eagles.

So, after centuries of a multitude of imaginary creations, an intelligent person surely must question why even the powerful want to believe in God.

Not only do people of all walks of life want to believe in God but they want to seek His help through prayer.

I suppose that we follow a religion in hopes of obtaining some divine help to solve our terrestrial stress. We pray for things and divine actions to reduce our troubles. Yet, the more we try to become religious, the more problems we seem to bring onto ourselves.

The world has divided itself into a multitude of religions and cultural faiths each claiming to be the only true one that will provide access to God and everlasting life.

However, I have noticed that the more some of these believe in the truth of their religion, the less they know about it. Recently, I took it upon myself to ask a Muslim friend why he asked (forced) his wife and eldest daughter to wear a hijab or specific Muslim head cover. He went into a tirade about how the Koran mandated such cover. So I took the time to read the Koran and research the topic. In fact, I also read the Bible and other holy books and

I have seen with my own eyes that those literary Do mandate a head cover. But they do NOT specify the fashion. So I went back and confronted my friend about it. I said, "Allah does mandate a cover but not the fashion. So why a hijab?...He was surprised. He did not have the answer to that other than to say "Well, it's the way it always been."

In other words the fashion was imposed by a culture. Not by God. And the culture mandated the fashion just to separate itself from others and identify itself as a group.

Over the centuries, this cultural religious thinking has used the word of God to separate itself, to create not love but hatred and it has become the source of war and discrimination between nations. This was not the intention of God.

"The belief in HEAVENLY salvation was instituted thousands of years ago by governments that needed to have willing soldiers die in the battlefield for EARTHLY conquests." – Sergio M. Pineda

So religious beliefs were instituted with two pillars of thought: Fear and hope. It became necessary to teach that one must FEAR an adversary but that through obedience and conformity to the existing leadership there would be HOPE of salvation.

In religion, the concept that God had to be feared but through submission there was hope for salvation. Or that there was an adversary - a Satan, a demon or a sin – that was to be feared but with obedience to the church there was hope for salvation.

The acceptance of this school of thought, has evolved into the basis of our political system as well. Our leaders use an eager communications media to present the worse of human nature. The ratings are high when an adversary is presented and the fear exaggerated. Every government presents an adversary – the communists, the dictators, the Terrorists, ISIS etc. This makes the potential political leader appear as a greater savior.

To this modern date, the teaching of acceptance in religious belief or political dogma is the best manner to control a repudiated population. Yet life does not have to be about constant struggle where we fear failure, shame or regret.

God is a God of life. He is the configuration of all atoms, living inside all things. God is capable of manipulating all matter and energy through you. In other words, God NEEDS YOU as a vehicle to alter and manipulate the material things around you so that your prayer can become effective.

Therefore, acceptance of your fears IS NOT something that God expects from you. God wants to see you save your life NOW!.. in THIS life!

"The Bible has one purpose only;
To gain favor with God so we may have His
favor on Earth." - Mike Murdock

If a person cannot save themselves in THIS life what makes them think the next life will be any better?

Many adhere to this, "make me feel good about my present condition" religious sermons, where they are told that acceptance of suffering in this life will lead to salvation. A bit like: "soldiers must die for their country", as opposed to "soldiers must win to save their country".

General Patton once said: "Don't die for your country...make the Enemy die for his country! That is what we do with effective prayer. We change our lives to WIN. We win NOW in THIS life. We make the evil that seeks to destroy us disappear from THIS life.

*"If every 8 year old in the world is taught meditation,
we will eliminate violence from the world within
one generation." - Dalai Lama*

In a small city in America's Midwest, a young girl named Aatifa grows up being taught strict Quranic customs. She attends the same school as Jane who grows up being taught strict Baptist rituals. Throughout their life they share the same city, the same school and the same government. But they never connect as individuals because religion separates them. All they know is that they are not the same because of religious dogma and family culture.

I find it almost incredible that from an early age we teach our children about religion but we fail to teach them wisdom. This religious form of teaching simply raises our children to be confused and angry in a divided world. The young girl that wears that hijab does not understand why she must adhere to such fashion or why she is attacked for wearing it. Neither does the young Christian child that was taught to believe in religious dogma over scientific fact.

We sometimes have a problem where we learn a lot of things, about other things, except about ourselves. We are busy in many things, except to take care of ourselves. We look at our outside problems but we never analyze ourselves. We seek happiness through acquisition of goods or pleasures without consideration for the happiness of others.

We become constrained by religion. We pay more attention to our priests, to our clothing, to our homes and not enough to our own selves. We refuse to seek a higher level of wisdom because we were taught that in doing so we were violating our religion and our culture. We end up believing how our religious leaders believe. Our thoughts not our own and our actions in life defined by others.

By looking to the outside only, we tend to blame others. We perceive erroneously that the fault of our problems is that we do not have the right clothing or the right car or the right conditions or people to give us those things.

One could say that the only way to bridge the two children in this Midwestern city is by converting both to atheism or by making both a lot wiser.

The communists tried at one time to eradicate religions and make all atheists. Religion was easy to replace with an all-powerful government but eclipsing God did not work because it's impossible to extinguish the internal flame that searches for answers that do not totally reside within us.

With wisdom we can alter our surrounding universe by simply refocusing our inner consciousness. Yes, by simply taking five minutes a day in the morning to PRAY and five minutes before bedtime to MEDITATE in our minds the events of that day. **The Secret to the life you want, to the goals you dream about, is hidden in this Daily Routine.**

Follow this disciplined routine until a habit is formed.

That simple exercise opens our inner consciousness and allows proper reflection of our life condition and purpose. This consciousness that we possess is our spirit and it has no religious affiliation. When we call on it in the name of God it becomes our Holy Spirit. Seek wisdom through it and will truly bind us regardless of any previous religious bigotry that was taught.

So, even today, when our lives enjoy more comfort, we are still surrounded by aggressive conditions and people that constantly undermine our prosperity. The search for wisdom and effective prayer will make us surmount those conditions and achieve a better level of prosperity.

The search for God is NOT a science project nor a matter of church attendance. Part of our problem in praying is that we look at God as some kind of invisible, extraterrestrial, old man flying around in the heavens. By religion standard God is supposed to look, think, feel and act as WE HUMANS perceive HIM. Religions create God to THEIR image and may assign him a racial profile or a sexuality. Regardless of religion, the dogma of the religion is what ends up being followed, and the believer only ends up having to accept the conditions for their misery.

Wisdom vs. Intelligence

> *It is not clear that intelligence has any*
> *long-term survival value" – Stephen Hawking*

I want to touch briefly on this difference because lately many intelligent people have been shown to fail in life with no apparent reason other than the public saying they are crazy or perverted.

These two human traits are not the same. Prisons are full of intelligent people that misused that intelligence to the detriments of others.

Wisdom should be used to enhance intelligence.

Wisdom is knowledge of Divinity without adhering to religious dogma. When God appeared to King Solomon and offered him anything, the king chose wisdom because by having wisdom he could have everything.

If you could summarize the entire Bible into one sentence you could say: In the Old Testament God created a perfect world for humans to live in, and in the New Testament Jesus shows that through wisdom we can solve ALL our problems.

Wisdom is acting with intelligence but analyzing with benevolence what cannot be seen or touched. A wise person questions his plans of action. In this manner that person is looking into the future. By doing this he looks beyond the intelligent solution and determines if his decisions will prevail the test of time.

In communist societies wisdom is not considered necessary. The leadership believes that a grounded education for all people makes an intelligent nation, and an intelligent nation would be powerful. This is wrong because intelligence is only the ability to comprehend and apply the practical and objective things that you have learned. In essence, it is only an ability to organize and although order is a pleasure it is not complete. Order needs the force of God to attain good and prevailing purpose.

Persons such as Attila, Napoleon, Stalin and Hitler were very intelligent but not very wise. Their infamy rests in the fact that their attempts to create and maintain power or prosperity led their nations to total destruction. By ignoring wisdom, they had created a lie; an impossible system to maintain that eventually crumbled, for themselves and for their nations. A man can be well organized in fighting a war, but what ORDER comes out from war? The Man's ability is in direct conflict with any prevailing long term fruitful purpose.

"Each generation imagines itself to be more intelligent than the one that went before it, and wiser than the one that comes after it" – George Orwell

How many times have we looked into our history and seen past intelligent people defend their past oppressions, or great military leaders whose wars never preserved their conquests. Or Leaders that wanted to preserve slavery and smart politicians that thought women had no common sense to vote. Not many today in our country will deny rights of liberty to minorities or women the way they were so intelligently explained by those leaders back then.

No empire that grew through war and was considered great in the past exists today.

Plenty of intelligence, but what was won? People and nations killed and died for short term gain and the problems of humanity continued.

"He who has no intelligence is happy with it" - S. African proverb

Intelligence is instinctive. Every life form has a certain amount of it to manage survival but is influenced by environment and education. Although scientists like the concept of judging species intelligence according to brain size, the truth is that red ants live better than some human tribes in Africa and Asia.

Wisdom, however, is a gift from God. The work of the unwise does not perpetuate because a technology can only be sustained and enhanced by wise persons. In those communist countries, many scientists had the intelligence to discover a new technology but lacked the wisdom to enhance it. And those who did have wisdom simply left their country and sneaked to free countries taking with them their knowledge.

5

THE LORD'S PRAYER

✠ ✠ ✠

*"A blazing fire makes flame and brightness out of everything
that is thrown into it"* – *Marcus Aurelius*

When the apostles asked Jesus to teach them how to pray, Jesus taught them this prayer, which is in effect a mini-gospel. No other prayer is necessary. No other prayer was taught.

So, it is not necessary to invent prayers to The Virgin Mary or to any particular saint. Do not waste your time invoking saints or angels. If any holy ghosts or entities act in your behalf it is because God mandated them. Jesus did not pray to any prophet or taught to his followers any other prayer. The Lord's Prayer is a very powerful holy invocation that gives thrust to your divine cycle.

The Lord's Prayer is a very powerful prayer. Throw your petitions into its fire. This prayer is a call for help to the Lord so that we may comply with a commitment. In doing so we also commit ourselves to The Lord, and the commitment is to follow your petition through the cycle of thought, words and actions.

When you pray it in silence, this prayer prepares your body, mind and soul to accept the challenges you will encounter along your cycle. This is a very personal preparation. God doesn't hear this silence.

When you pray it aloud along with your petitions, even the stones will hear you, and the environment around you will prepare itself to help your purpose.

When you act on the petitions made, all matter, energy and space of the universe becomes your tool and resource to help you.

And when you work with The Lord's Prayer in mind, you and your organization develop the momentum of a moving train.

And your objective will come to pass.

So, whether I pray at church or in private, I pray in this manner:

Our Father YAHWE
Who reigns over the
Heavens and the Earth
Hallowed be your name

God has a holy name. Do not confuse Him with other gods or situations. Call Him the way you would address a very important person.

Your kingdom come
And your will be done
On Earth as it is in Heaven

We acknowledge that ALL things are possible to God and therefore only He can place those resources at our disposition. Furthermore, we offer ourselves as the vehicle through which He can act to make these petitions a reality.

Give us each day our daily bread. Forgive us our sins as we also forgive those who sin against us.

We ask that all our daily worthwhile activities be rewarded. That our daily necessities be provided for so that during the realization of our daily activity we may not trample on someone else's prosperity

And keep us from temptation

We ask God to help us maintain our focus. And to remove from our path any items, situations, or persons that may deviate us from our objective.

And deliver us from all evil

We ask that all evil persons, bad actions or misfortune factors be set apart from us. So we may not become the consequence of someone else's cycle. Here, it is important to specify in detail what evil things you want to be cleared of.

Providing us with health,

wisdom and prosperity...

> Specify your petition. Whether it is for a particular health, wisdom or monetary issue.

And further Father YAHWE...
(ask, don't be afraid, ask repeatedly)

> Repeat your prayer with your specific petition at least seven times. This repetitive petition process will help you establish exactly where your mind needs to focus.
>
> If you are Christian, praying alongside a friend, follow the recommendation of Jesus and make your petition in the name of Jesus Christ. By doing this you acknowledge Jesus message of personal empowerment.

This we ask in the name of Jesus Christ.

This invocation is a simple, but extremely powerful step it should be made before you start any project or cycle. It will give you the necessary personal control so that you will not stray from your final objective.

In other words, the Lord's Prayer has the power to bring into you what is known as FAITH. And faith is the secondary step that will bring about the enthusiasm to take the correct actions.

6

THOUGHTS ABOUT PRAYER

✠ ✠ ✠

"The greatest discovery of our generation is that human beings can alter their lives by altering their attitudes of mind. As you think, so shall you be." - William James

The prayer starts with a thought. Any thought. Sometimes the greatest feats accomplished start with a really silly thought. A genius is someone who dares to carry a silly thought over a cycle and prove that it could be completed. So is a madman.

"Only those who attempt the absurd, Will achieve the impossible" - M.C. Escher

Traveling to distant planets or visiting the bottom of our oceans were initially crazy thoughts. Whether it was Julius Verne or Hollywood movies, all the genius or crazy actions of humanity have started with a thought.

But when our thoughts turn to prayers it is because the right way of thinking is incomplete and we need spiritual help to focus our purpose. We find ourselves with a problem or in a situation that we do not have an answer to. A person will start to ponder,

"What am I doing here", "What is going on with my life", "What should I do about this".

With these questions a person starts to evaluate his own worth. Sometimes, the evaluation is not positive because things are not going well. A sense of guidance - from anyone - is sought. In most cases, this is the time when a small amount of prayer is done with no results. There is really no plan of action to remedy the situation.

But to think right and be able to find an answer, one must always remember why we want to be alive. Understanding our purpose sets our process of thought correctly.

Wisdom only requires the capacity of being honest with yourself. To ask yourself the simplest and yet the toughest questions about your own character, your purpose in life and what you really, really want.

"Children must be taught how to think,
Not what to think." – Margaret Mead

The easiest way to discover one's sense of purpose in life is to ask a child. I did this with my infant son. Hoping to capture his future ambitions, I asked: *"What would you like to do?"* and with a great angelic smile he simply answered, *"I would like to play".*

At first I reacted with sarcasm to his innocent answer. - "Yeah, don't we all" - Seconds later I grasped its immense wisdom. In that answer I discovered why God had placed Adam in paradise; so that the spirit, living inside a material body could pass the time playing and in his game find happiness. Regardless of age, we all want to constantly play and the game we choose is our purpose.

When a child is learning how to walk and falls down 50 times, they never think to themselves, "Maybe this isn't for me".

"When I was 5 years old, my mother always told me
That happiness was the key to life. When I went to school,
They asked me what I wanted to be when I grew up. I wrote
down: 'Happy'. They told me I didn't understand the assignment,
and I told them they didn't understand life". – John Lennon

As shallow as that may seem, God created such a playpen for us. Adam and Eve had received an opportunity to pass their time in playfulness, raising their descendants in a wonderful place. Through the use of materials, the human spirit was provided with the ability to create tools and toys that would make life a fun game. No borders, no nationalities, and no hate. In exchange, God asked for two simple things from Adam and Eve, LOVE and LOYALTY.

Mankind let Him down.

Adam and his family were expelled from paradise, but his purpose in life did not change. Happiness was still to be pursued but now humans had to play a rough game. One in which a person would seek happiness in the company of others, while at the same time facing constant obstacles. Unfortunately, other persons would create most of these obstacles, by creating boundaries, religions, classes and hatred.

And this is why we pray. To establish a communication with God by which we can obtain help in influencing positively the result of dealing with others.

The game of life is difficult to understand, because we do not like the difference between playfulness and discipline. But all games are played in a court that is defined by objects, endurance, rules, and time. Without these markers, the game of life would cease to be an interesting game, and life would become abuse.

We lost our chance to live in paradise and now we have to build the park in which we want to play within our own community. It is up to each one of us to create our playing field. We have the opportunity to choose who we want to play with and where. And breaking the rules creates an abusive environment that we call war.

The playing field is established by the way we think. Each country or society will organize differently according to how we are taught to think.

> *"Most people think it takes a long time to change.*
> *It doesn't. Change is immediate! Instantaneous!*
> *It may take a long time to decide to change…but change*
> *happens in a heartbeat!". – Andy Andrews.*

Our mind is like a nebula, full of potential energy, where all of a sudden an idea pops up like a star. These thoughts are a sudden flash. They can become actions in a very short time. The way we construct these ideas is the way we build our society.

In the previous chapter, we realized the importance of values to create affinity within our own community. Values become the local rules in the game that we play within our society. But, because values are self-imposed, the harder the rules, the harder we make the game. Some societies impose on themselves very intolerant rules. We all become quite frustrated when we see an intolerant referee stop the game at all moments. The players get tired, the viewers get bored and in time even the referees get despaired. Trying to keep order in the field through punishment eventually gets old. People will revolt. So the rules must be designed as fine lines that protect equilibrium between fun and despair.

*"Peace cannot be kept by force. It can
only be achieved by understanding" – Albert Einstein*

The thought of happiness can only be achieved if we are happy with ourselves and within our nation. Our values cannot be in place to hurt, but only to restrict abuse. Given this condition, the game of life can be an enjoyable episode of being yourself, doing what you desire while acquiring the items that make you happy.

The summary of our purpose in life: to BE, to DO and to HAVE in our game is why we learn how to pray. To attain these three things in the proper way by playing in the right manner, with Gods guidance and help in what sometimes becomes rough or even violent and worst of all, in a life where we MUST play. There is no option, if you are alive you ARE in some sort of game.

A sense of purpose

I do not want to dwell in the topic of purpose too long, because it is a theme discussed every day by other philosophers and self-help authors, that have explored it better in a more effective manner. I only want to address certain pragmatic issues that pertain to the praying process.

*"A mind that is stretched by new experiences,
Can never go back to its old dimensions". –
Oliver Wendell Holmes Jr.*

If the main purpose of mankind is to BE someone, to DO something with your time, and to HAVE something in your life, then these are the dynamics of the Divine Cycle.

To the person that prays I ask: In this prayer Who are you? What can you do? What do you want?

What you play in life is your doing. How and what you do, will produce what you can have.

Let us take a microscopic view of these three facets. The first one is to look at us as a being. Most of us hate to look inside. It is here where we usually become our worst critics because we dislike the effort of maintaining our weight, our health and our values.

Happiness is hard to achieve when what pleases the body sometimes hurts the mind, and vice-versa. We pray to find the correct balance between what we want to be and what we do because this determines what we will end up with.

Your body is a precious machine

"Physical fitness is not only one of the most important keys to a healthy body, it is the basis of dynamic and creative intellectual activity". – John F. Kennedy

Our body is the greatest gift God has given the spirit. Through the body the spirit is now able to DO things. Man could be a creator and manipulate matter and energy which are the main elements of the entire universe. By doing this, God gave mankind the ability to become His partner and expand the process of creation.

The body of a person is more than a sophisticated machine; it is a creative vehicle. Inside your mind, resides the spirit, your eternal being, which needs this vehicle to act and create in a material world. If you do not believe in this just look at a dead person. The dead are like abandoned cars in an impound lot, with no owner to make them run. Jesus was able to restart one of these "vehicles" -Lazarus- by asking the spirit of Lazarus to return and re-take possession of the body that had been assigned to him. The Bible does not tell us whether Lazarus enjoyed the experience of having to take back his used body, but Jesus action demonstrates the primary importance of the spirits' ability to operate inside and outside the body. Many doctors have resurrected people that were already thought dead. In all cases, it is proof that the body is a vehicle entered by the spirit when it is useful, and when the vehicle fails, the spirit exits.

"How long are you going to wait before
You demand the best for yourself." - Epictetus

If you refuse to take care of this body vehicle, entrusted to you for a short time, you set in motion a series of poor cycles. This is because the result of your prayer is proportionate to the condition of your body. You need a good vehicle to do a good task.

Let's say, that a person whom smokes, pays little attention to his diet or to himself, prays effectively to receive a promotion, although he knows that once he receives this promotion his better job requires more traveling, longer working hours, and additional stress.

What this individual has done by pursuing his Prayer Cycle for a promotion, is place himself in a position of physical danger. His body's condition will not be ready to handle the task produced by his praying. He has decided to carry a load on inadequate equipment.

Conversely, not paying attention to building a strong mind converts the body into a depreciable machine that is used by other individuals to execute menial tasks. The person that executes the labor is not as valuable as the person who thinks out the labor. The human spirit thinks out the labor, but knows that the body is a replaceable vehicle.

Subsequently, to have a good life in this world, the spirit uses the mind and the body to complete cycles of our thoughts, words, work, and achievement before its eventual wear out. And it is the merit and magnitude of these cycles that determine the quality of life for each individual.

But, like any machine, our bodies' decay, so we seek relief from the constant wear and tear. Surviving like other animals is not sufficient for the human spirit. We must use our creativity to obtain comfort. Notice, for example, that our biggest industries are based in creating or doing things others need or want to alleviate effort. This alleviation of effort ensures a greater sense of survival. Imagine for a minute, going back to an era where cars or planes did not exist as tools to ease transportation. Or where heavy machinery was nonexistent to soften the strain of construction. These were the ages when labor was difficult, lifestyle conditions were poor and as a result the value placed on life was sometimes not very high.

"There is a way to do it better – find it" – Thomas Edison

The person, who can create something to alleviate effort, shall become prosperous.

We were given as a species the unique ability to create and re-create anything that we can conceptualize to adapt to any environment. Furthermore, God gave each individual the capacity to be unique in the way he or she can create. A way to create wealth is simply to satisfy a need for comfort.

Back in the 1960's and '70's it was almost wicked to be a materialistic person or to strive to have possessions. But in reality, that is the only way the human being can survive. We do not have the powerful limbs and muscles of other animals, or their ferocious size and teeth to defend ourselves. The only thing that guarantees our supremacy as a species is the ability to transform matter, energy and space into tools. Creation is nothing more than the application of energy towards a purpose.

There is nothing wrong with being materialistic. The reason material things become important and we become attached to them is because it takes great energy to fashion them and great effort to acquire them within a limited period of time. A material thing is a reflection of work.

Therefore, this continuous flow of energy will act by the direction of man or by directive of nature. Either way it is a cause of God.

"My life seemed to be a series of events and accidents. Yet when I look back I see a pattern." - Benoit B. Mandelbrot

How you direct this flow of energy determines the outcome of your Divine Cycles. Of the three capacities - to be, to do and to have- the **most interesting** is the ability **to do**; your work. People are very interested in knowing if you are an actor or a scientist or a pastor etc., and what you do at work. Through work you find the best answers to your prayers. Your purpose is to work in a capacity to direct your daily energy. This capacity justifies your existence, plays an important role in how compatible of a person you are, and determines the quantity and quality of what you will accomplish in this life. This is why, when we meet someone for the first time, we want to know as soon as possible what that person does for a living.

The **most important** of the capacities is to BE. This is the way you think about the personal result of your prayer. Asking yourself: "who really am!", What is my character"? "Who/what am I trying to become?"

Whereas action and work take time and discipline, the perception of your own being can be changed in a flash. You can stop seeing yourself as a loser and immediately see yourself as winning. Which means that your cycles or any course of events that are happening with your life can be changed as fast as you can change your mind.

> *"Immense power is acquired by assuring yourself*
> *in your secret reveries that you were born to*
> *control affairs"' - Andrew Carnegie*

Remember: You can change the direction of your life in a flash because you can find God in a flash.

God does not impose harsh terms on those who seek Him. God is ALL. He is available in the manner in which YOU want to perceive Him. You can choose your own concept of God.

Just look inside and ask yourself "Who am I"? There, in answering that question you will find the power of God that only requires being true ONLY to yourself.

If you are going to live according to how someone else thinks of you, you are going to be like a gladiator, thrown into the battle, – by others - without consultation.

When you feel trapped in a terrible place or a terrible job or an unhappy relationship, you can always request a change to a different place, with different people and in a different environment and this request can be made in a flash, with a simple change of mind.

All you need to know is your abilities and trust those abilities and let God overcome your limitations.

Just make the request happen. Jesus mandated; *"ask and thou shall receive"*. And this is why prayer happens.

One of my favorite sports is snow skiing. It is astonishingly similar to our life. What they show you before your ski adventure is perfect. They show beautiful photographs of the cotton colored mountains and trees. In a video you notice elegant skiers that slide in perfect harmony and total enjoyment, bouncing softly on the downhill powder.

But the reality is quite different.

Initially, you arrive to a cold world. You must pay regardless of experience, participation or whether you are on the way up or coming down. You must learn, and also adapt quickly to survive. If you went there with relatives, the entire family disperses all over the place with each member choosing a different run. If you fall, very few will be there to help you. In fact, as you drop, most skiers, even your friends, will make an effort to avoid you. If you did not receive instruction the trees will teach or stop you with painful impacts.

On top of the mountain, as you face the challenge of negotiating the way down, you realize that only your ability and learning facilitates the possibility that you will successfully complete the run. If you learned well, the game will be under your control, you will have a fun time, and prosper physically. A bad student is in for a miserable time.

Similarly, the search to discover who you are or what you will be, is a lonely trip. You cannot depend on someone else. No one will guarantee you happiness. As a player you must take the time to learn, train, and practice. This way, you will learn what works for YOU.

Along the way, you will discover your true friends and separate them from party buddies. That which brings you prosperity, you will hold on to dearly and care for, and eventually you will dismiss all those people and things that represent a liability to your wellbeing.

Happiness is the constant pursuit of prosperity; the ability to play the game of life without being destroyed by painful moments.

Maintaining prosperity and happiness is a matter of continuously completing cycles that make you a better being.

Therefore, a Divine cycle that produces an Effective Prayer is thinking about a goal and then doing or not doing something about it. It is a decision that carries a commitment. Whatever is done affects the elements of matter, space, energy and time and when a thing is done with purpose or creativity, one can say that there is control of such a cycle because you are in control of these elements.

"Once you make a decision the universe conspires to make it happen". - Ralph Waldo Emerson

In this book, the winner is the one who learns how to pray and the person that knows how to complete Divine Cycles.

Success in a prayer is the completion of a cycle according to your expectation.

Every day, take a few minutes and follow these five steps to set your mind in the correct thought process:

1. Visualize what you are praying for. What is your petition, why and when you need it. Visualize it, think it, and daydream it as precisely as possible.
2. Think who are the persons you need to reach with your prayers to achieve results. Remember that the answer to your prayer may rest in your ability to satisfy someone else's concern.
3. Visualize a better you, seeking wisdom and being healthy so that you may never find yourself overwhelmed.
4. Think creatively knowing that your decisions can be changed at any time allowing you to correct any errors.
5. Think of a way to be thankful for your success by praying for others and offering them a piece of pleasure.

7

HOW TO TALK

✚ ✚ ✚

"Mankind's greatest achievements have come about by talking, and its greatest failures by not talking". – Stephen Hawking

The word(s) that you speak is a simple, but extremely powerful step to be made before you start any project or cycle. It will give you the necessary personal control so that you will not stray from your final objective.

There was a time in which the Church would penalize profanity with death because they knew that words were the creative or destructive force of our universe.

Words have life! They become live once uttered. They create feelings of love or purpose or hatred. They produce action and reaction. They become YOU!

YOU are a prayer that was answered to your progenitor. You lived in nothingness until your mother called you.

"The Word became flesh and resided among us"' - John 1:14

Hence, God ordered that man should follow THE WORD!
It has become customary to use all sorts of heinous words in

our daily vocabulary and yet we are surprised when life becomes hell.

You are YOUR words and other people see you as WORDS.

When you thought of yourself (in the previous chapter), what word(s) did you see?... Did you see kind?, affable?, honest?, prosperous?, or did you see angry?, disgusted?, forgotten?...

What words would other people use when they think of you?

In a universe of atoms that are mostly space, and react to the most minimal vibration, words are the cause of such vibration.

You are the product of words and EVERYTHING that surrounds you is the product of words. Silence never brought about any material creation.

Be careful with your words. Be aware of the power that can come from your words.

"In our thoughts and words, we create our own weaknesses and our own strengths". Betty Eadie

Even when you speak to yourself, follow up with the Lord's Prayer.

The Lord's Prayer has the power to bring into you what is known as FAITH. And faith is the secondary step that will bring about the enthusiasm to take the correct actions.

My system of prayer is very personal but has served me well. I bought a small ring notebook, which I call my book of prayers. It allows me to track each cycle. In difference to a dairy, where people write about their immediate past, my book of prayer is one in which I write about my immediate future. What I do is write each one of my prayer objectives at the top of each blank page. I dedicate one page to each prayer. In the cover of the notebook I have pasted The Lord's Prayer, which I slowly read and to which I add the written petitions. By now I have many of these notebooks.

I am ambitious and I have asked for a lot, albeit of remorse. Throughout the page I write my process of thought. Basically, what I do is convert my vision into written words and develop a critical route of how to get to my objective. These written words when accompanied by the Lord's Prayer as a prefix commence a powerful process of invocation. The petitions always come about. So, every morning when I sit and write my new prayer, I am writing down my destiny. I already know my immediate future.

"I AM, two of the most powerful words.
For what you put after them shapes your reality." - Joel Osteen

Every morning as I wake up I visualize a cross and I think out The Lord's Prayer. If I am still lying down I may soon find myself again relaxing myself to sleep. But as I wake up I continue thinking and then saying the Lord's Prayer. What I have done in effect is started the day with a thought and a word process that clears my mind and soothes my spirit. I feel I am ready to meet my destiny. Since destiny is a continuation of a cycle that started with a thought, I wait to see who are the people I communicate with in the next moments. Sometimes a message comes into my mind, like a line in an old Teletype. Or sometimes it is the first call outside of my home that sets the tone or the message for what is to happen during the rest of the day. The words and events that are discussed in that first conversation with someone else are the continuation of a cycle that you must become aware of so that you may take the right actions.

That first line or thought that comes into my mind or my first conversation will be telling me: this is a day to "remember my family" or "finish incomplete task(s) or "be aware of temptations today". No matter what the conversation was about, it sets the pattern for the day.

As night follows the day, the word will follow the thought. The cycle is not reversible; it must be completed and re-started.

A friend of mine came in one night and said: "I had a terrible day. I should have gone back to bed when I spilled my coffee this morning". As it turns out, that morning she got an early call from a co-worker advising her that an expected client would not be arriving that day. My friend became frustrated she was hoping to close an important deal with this customer that morning. Her thoughts became confused; she dropped the coffeepot for lack of paying attention and almost burned herself. She hurriedly got dressed and left in her new car towards the office. To avoid traffic she took a different route through an industrial park. One she thought would be a shortcut. On the way it started to rain and unknowing hit a pothole causing damage to the front end of her car. While waiting for the wrecker the rain increased to the point of flooding the entire street. She finally abandoned her car and walked back home in the rain.

I told her that in the morning that first call from her co-worker was a message to "Do not hurry-Another time will come". It was not that she would not get the contract, but that on such specific day the contract was not to be gotten. But by becoming angry and frustrated she had not stopped to think that her hurried lifestyle was not going to get her anywhere. Instead of analyzing that first conversation, and interpreting its positive message, she started a frantic cycle that got her in trouble.

When you pray you <u>always</u> get a message. Be wise so that you may discover its positive implications.

I write down my petitions. I have a business journal in which at the top of each page I have written the name of each one of my clients. I write down the potential amount of work that I may do for them and I even write down a short idea on how to approach each one of them. On the cover of this book I have pasted The

Lord's Prayer. Every day, when I review my journal I read out aloud, or pray, The Lord's Prayer. Then, I commence writing my notes on the book.

In doing this, what I have done is think about my client(s) with The Lord in mind and then I have followed with words. I tell you that regardless of national economic ups and downs that client list has been enough to provide me with luxury.

Few years ago, I dreamt of living by the ocean. And not just in a simple house or apartment with a view of the water. I wanted a mansion, like the ones those Hollywood stars have in southern California with the front yard caressed by the waves. So at the top of the blank page I wrote something like:

Petition: *"I am to acquire a large home by the beach, Mediterranean architecture, as I envision it, within 1 year."*

Then below I wrote:

P of T: (This is my **P**rocess of **T**hought or my plan of action to acquire this petition.)

I knew this petition was really ambitious. First of all, I did not have the money. I had just come out of a divorce almost penniless, but after writing the petition and invoking God by reciting The Lord's Prayer, a voice, deep inside, told me that this petition would be granted.

My plan of action got stuck many times. And it took me more than a year. But every time I was stuck, it was because I needed something extraordinary to help me. So I would develop a petition seeking help on **that particular** situation. In time, I had many petitions that where part of getting to the original petition of acquiring the house. But I kept the cycle alive by praying, verbalizing it and acting on it. Soon the money and all the resources arrived, and from the most unexpected persons and places.

"Words are containers for power,
You choose what kind of power they carry." - Joyce Meyer

Words have a way to become Matter. Be careful of how you speak. The Apostles Paul and James would warn to be careful of what was said. *"To tame the tongue, we must recognize its power for good or for evil."*

Your prosperity, your blessings and good will can be traced to careful and wise words spoken throughout the history of your life.

By the same token, every disease you carry, every misfortune that besets you and your loved ones can be traced to words that came out of you and those who surround you and took a life of their own and became a reality. Your anger, your insults, your rudeness, your careless words flung about, that you thought meant nothing when they were said, but were uttered frequently, were like seeds of horror sowed into your field of life.

Jesus himself said" *But I tell you that every careless word that people speak, they shall give an accounting for it in the day of judgement. For by your words you will be justified, and by your words you will be condemned."*

Your day of judgement is not the day of your death. **It is the day in which you receive the answer to your prayers!**

8

THE ACTION EMPOWERS
THE WORD.
✠ ✠ ✠

"Apply yourself to thinking through difficulties – hard times can be softened, tight squeezes widened, and heavy loads made lighter. You always have a move to make, there is always something you can do. Even if that move is just making your peace." - Seneca

How to act

I recently watched on a television documentary a story about the thousands of miserable people that are born, live, and die inside the great garbage dumps of cities such as Mumbai or Manila. I started to wonder if God would ever listen to these people's prayers. How could they be so forsaken? But I realized that all of the poor people that dwelled in the dump lived there because they were accustomed to that lifestyle. None of these long-term residents had a strong determination to get out of there. Therefore, their prayers and petitions were confined to that garbage universe. The possibility of living outside that world seemed too distant for them. In fact these people are afraid of any change that could displace them out of such environment, they are accustomed to this world.

Attempting to move the homeless from under a bridge, into a shelter is not an easy task. Any city official will tell you that the job usually becomes conflictive, expensive and unappreciated. It is not that the "bums" want to live out in the open. They are afraid of anything else; living precariously is all they know.

Usually this fear that holds us back is a state of ignorance, apathy or an addiction. It gives us a false sense of security. Whether the addiction is to drugs, alcohol, food, work or anything, it maintains us in a self-destruction universe.

The effective prayer not only has the right value, technology, and invocations, it must also have faith. Faith is the personal knowledge that you use to carry out a task or project to completion without having all necessary resources at hand from the beginning. You must translate this faith into a proper visual thought by believing you can realize your dream. Then, you must speak or write down in words what we want to accomplish and explain to God and to other persons how we need their help.

In some cases you may have to be quite insistent on your request. But the help will be offered. It is up to you to convert this help into action.

Faith is the knowledge and feeling of self-empowerment, but it must follow the first two steps of visualizing and speaking.

To act without taking these two steps first is to act impulsively, and this can start a cycle of self-destruction.

Similarly to building a house, effective faith is the third building block after having accomplished the first two steps.

Sometimes we feel that we have faith, or that we pray enough, or that we go to church sufficiently and this satisfies our spiritual needs. But in reality those feelings are simply a personal form of therapy. But those feelings will not help you much in accomplishing a specific objective, because those feelings come and go in a disoriented manner. They become mood swings that affect our actions, and disorganized actions are conducive to downward forms of behavior.

Jesus said: *"Ask and you shall receive"*. With this statement he was saying: "Verbalize your petition to all parties who will listen and who can help you". Sometimes when you make your presentation, you receive the attention and help from the most unsuspected sources.

So, let's imagine for a moment that one of those girls who lives in anguish at the garbage dump is not happy and really wants to get out. What would be the scenario of a successful Divine Cycle for this person?

The first part of the process for her effective prayer would be to start visualizing a life outside the dump. Because when you are absolutely destitute and you have absolutely no money, you still have YOURSELF. All improvement starts WITHIN YOU. If you improve the vision of yourself you have started your rise towards the stars. So, the minute she thinks about leaving that wasteland, she has begun a cycle. The second step for her is to pray in the manner described in the previous chapter; petition The Lord for help and guidance and detailing as best as possible her plans for starting the new life she is visualizing. This second step is a direct telephone call to God. God <u>will</u> hear that prayer and place before that person, the proper individuals, elements and conditions that will enable this person to act. The opportunity will show up. The person must then make it clear to these other individuals that she needs their help to get out of that place.

This person has now fueled the Divine Cycle of an Effective Prayer. She must maintain the momentum, because if she does not take the opportunity that presented itself, the energy of the cycle will be broken and the person will never leave the dump. Faith must be inserted here, at this juncture. And it must be inserted with boldness. Otherwise, all this individual would do is create a cycle that maintains her within the garbage.

"Making a bold move is the only way to truly advance toward the grandest vision the universe has for you" - Oprah Winfrey

In other words, any individual has the freedom to create his or her own cycle. Acting according to the process and thereby controlling the cycle or not regulating the cycle through omission or laziness. The result is known as destiny.

So the third step is FAITH. To act. And to act boldly. To base your actions with the belief that you can do what you planned. Take your belief and put it into words and then to act on it. Faith is to trust in God and act on your thoughts.

I understand that apathy and addictions are hard to escape from, making faith a difficult thing to accomplish. But I know from personal experience, that only by praying "The Lord's Prayer" you can attain effective development of mental strength. Only by praying can you find the courage to act positively to blast off towards any objective or to get out of personal torture.

Belief, Trust and Faith

Many times I have heard a multitude of relatives and friends say that after they make a petition to God they trust in the fact that He will comply with their request. They pray like crazy, then the years go by and their expectations are always short filled. What has happened with these individuals is that they confused Trust with Faith.

Faith without work is dead. Faith in God is not the same as Trust in God. Faith in God is trust placed INTO ACTION!

"A man can succeed at almost anything
For which he has unlimited enthusiasm" - Charles M. Schwab

There is a great difference between believing in God, trusting in God and having faith in God. Most humans believe in a God or Gods, because they realize that life is a composition of elements that no single individual can direct just by him or herself. Therefore, many, including myself, believe that our individual spirits can belong to no one except a greater spiritual being. If it were not this way, then, humans could infuse life into any rock just the same way that God created human life out of dust.

Faith is a process of discovery.

For materialistic persons, sometimes only by seeing and touching items, we can believe that something is real. But not all reality is tangible. Gravity for example, is a reality. Friction is a reality, Lift is a reality, and Impact is a reality. These things always have existed, yet it took centuries for mankind to comprehend them. They are laws of physics that cannot be challenged easily without taking mortal risk. And the more we study science, we discover that physics, which is not obvious to the eye, is the inalterable law of God, that rules not only matter, space and energy, but also the relationship between human beings. In other words, it rules the objective and the abstract.

Our universe is an infinite game of discovery. We play with items and situations for centuries only to discover that we always had at hand the answer to our dreams. Since the dawn of mankind there was a dream to fly. It takes only a few pieces of curved wood and some cloth to craft a wing. And although mankind had these items for thousands of years, and even used them as sails to harness the power of the wind at sea, it took the vision of two brothers from Ohio to give it the twist of Lift. Had the Wright brothers left their sticks and canvas folded in a shelf of their bicycle shop, humanity would probably still be mocking the concept of flying. Flight was an act of faith by someone who had discovered what all along was so obvious but yet unseen simply because they believed that it was there.

Your solutions are out there, just not visible yet. We are surrounded by the solutions to our problems, and by the elements to build our dreams. But it is usually difficult to see the things that we need and how we need to apply them. Trusting and acting on your instincts is an act of faith that can create a miracle.

A miracle is a scientific fact.

A miracle is nothing more than the ability to manipulate the atomic particles that are in activity inside all items, to obtain a desired result. We know this is possible. We discussed earlier how quantum physics, shows the result of a given experiment can vary according to the expectation of the scientist performing the experiment. Therefore, the same experiment performed different scientists can render multiple results.

Everything is composed of atoms that are in constant movement. The human eye has never seen an atom. Yet we know it is there, unseen, and humans are even capable of manipulating its energy in a most explosive manner.

Sometimes the unseen solution shows itself by study, or through consultation with others, and many times because we acted, and as we worked the solutions appeared by "coincidence". But this coincidence is in reality God's intervention rewarding your faith.

I personally believe that life exists in this planet because of

Divine intervention and not because of an accident of nature. Here on Earth, life forms exist in the most unreachable, and inhospitable of places such as inside toxic volcanoes, in the extreme ocean depths, in the highest and coldest of mountains. And life here in these extremes not only survives but also prospers. Life forms on Earth are compositions of mostly carbon and other chemical elements that have a tremendous ability to adapt to the surrounding environment. If life is simply a chemical reaction that adapts itself to any environment, then some life form should have adapted itself in the Moon or in Venus or in all of the other planets. But life does not exist in the Moon or in Venus or any of those planets, because there has been no Divine decision for it to exist over there.

Trust is not enough.

Similarly, when we say that we trust in God we simply trust that God is God. It is just an act of acknowledgement. To God it is not important whether we believe or trust in Him. After all, God was God billions of years before the first apparition of a man over the face of this planet. What is important for Him and for us humans is that through faith we may obtain His help to prosper. To prosper as a human is to carry out the work of God.

I believe and I trust, however, the fact that it was God who organized the elements that were in the "shelf" of this planet.

Life is an act of faith from God. This is an axiom of physics.

Belief and trust are parts of "thought" and "word" in the Divine Cycle. Faith is action.

With all our problems and challenges of life, it is just a matter of figuring out how we can solve things. The answer to all our questions is not yes or no. It is **HOW?**

How can I build a better business?
How can I restore my health?

How can I improve my relationships?
How can I get a better job?

All the raw material elements have already been provided to satisfy our dreams. It is through faith that we must discover the unseen "How".

When you ask yourself a question, your process of thought and meditation has started. Then, your answers will present themselves as you pray using words. Once present, your faith will guide you to the positive result you are expecting.

Therefore, our relationship with God is not simply one of Sunday adoration. It is a relationship of faith in our work and in our life's decisions so that we may carry out a mission of prosperity every day.

Many people who consider themselves "saved" or "Born Again" after becoming believers in Jesus, confuse the message of personal salvation because the saving does not take place in just the belief in Jesus, but in acting and keeping in mind the pursuit of prosperity for the benefit of their neighbor.

Never confuse Faith in God with belief or trust in God. FAITH is your beliefs and the trust you have in God placed into good ACTIONS.

"Everything comes to him
who hustles while he waits" – Thomas Edison

In an address at Tabor Academy, my beloved prep school, USS CONSTITUTION Commander William F. Foster Jr. USN recounted an incredible story of faith placed into action.

"Sometime during the War of 1812, the plans for a coastal voyage betrayed, "Old Ironsides" sailed into a trap: a fleet of British warships awaited her as she made her way up the Jersey

shore. With disaster about to strike, the wind died. All ships lay becalmed awaiting a deadly battle. With the fleet of equally motionless British vessels poised in the horizon, The Captain ordered the anchor chain lowered into a long boat, rowed forward and dropped. Sailors hauled the mighty tall ship the length of the chain, pulled the anchor and lowered it once more into the long boat to start the process all over again. Relentlessly, for over thirty continuous hours, the great ship inched her way through a glassy sea until the wind arose; but by then, by great labor she had gained sufficient seaway distance to slip from the British trap".

When things looked bleak, the men of the USS CONSTITUTION had acted on the thoughts, words and faith of their Captain. They had saved themselves physically and spiritually and probably they had saved their nation. Faith had come to the Captain from wisdom, which made him see that under that specific circumstance, pulling a chain for thirty agonizing hours was a less painful and more courageous alternative than facing fifteen minutes of battle.

Actions with faith are actions of courage. With faith you soon realize that your thoughts and words produce reactions on other individuals. It makes you and everyone around start to think about your topic of concern. Some people will help you, and others will envy you. But your ongoing cycle cannot be stopped by anyone but by you.

Faith is the force that covers the entire Divine Cycle of an Effective Prayer, just like the atmosphere that covers our planet. Everything in this universe exists because it was an act of someone's faith. At first it was an act of faith by God. Then, He gave humans the same capacity of action.

But how does faith arrive?

It arrives by taking action. **Any action done with self-confidence.**

Success does not belong to the good nor to the hard working. **It belongs to the bold!**

Whenever I traveled with my Mom and we found ourselves in a tight spot, she would say to me: "Well, do something". Now I realize that those words meant "Act with faith now".

When you start acting, faith develops its own momentum. After that first action is taken, it is all a matter of persistence.

"There are many talented people who haven't
fulfilled their dreams because they over thought it,
or were too cautious, and were unwilling to
make the leap of faith" - James Cameron

The most incredible act of faith in recent history is the call by President Kennedy, to land a man on the Moon before 1970. With a speech at Rice University in Houston, he challenged the American people to design, invent, and re-create systems, metals, fuels, and processes, most non-existent at the time, in order to travel to a celestial body that humanity had only seen as a pagan god for centuries before.

Earth to the Moon...what a 238,900 miles non-stop leap of Faith!

The speech was the verbalization of a dream that had existed for decades before, but that had remained only as magic thought to be exploited only by writers and moviemakers. But, after the speech, the entire nation acted. Metals, fuels and processes appeared. In 1969, less than a decade after the Rice University speech, two human beings arrived safely at the surface of the Moon.

Throughout the adventure, many tough obstacles were encountered, but the result was never in doubt. It is important to mention that at all times, before rocket launches, prayer and petitions were made. The participants never forgot God. The nation had postulated the idea of traveling to the moon and had acted with faith to accomplish its goal.

This trip made the entire world believe that anything was possible. It was possible because Americans started to apply their beliefs in space travel towards discovering what was there, but unseen.

It was a matter of taking a posture of persistent action rather than passive acceptance in dealing with any challenge encountered. Everything is possible, but only for those who persist in the process of the Divine Cycle. It becomes worthwhile BEING someone, who can DO something that can HAVE value.

Your prayer needs DEVOTION

This shows your level of commitment. Devotion is the complement to the ACTION step. Devotion is nothing more than a commitment and a sense of duty in carrying out the cycle that you have started.

This level of commitment is the power towards your objective. Devotion is persistent work. But it is not toil or simple labor.

Work is the repetitive task in which you dedicate your thoughts, words, your actions and that must be created and recreated until the cycle is perfected.

In business terms, an idea cannot be productive, or be deserving of merit, if it stays simply as an unrealized idea. It must be worked until it becomes tangible and the work requirement to go from idea to successful product is devotion.

In effective prayer there is such a thing called "timing". Although the dimension of time is totally different to God as it is to humans, God knows that the time at which a prayer is answered makes all the difference in the world to a human. The level of commitment that you have to a specific cause determines an answer to your prayer at the proper time. Very much like a pass in a football game; you can ask that the prayer be passed on to you at a certain moment, but you must be there to receive the benefit when the angels of The Lord come to you. Otherwise it is going to be either a missed shot or a fumble. Every time you ask, God's quarterback will throw you the pass. **You have to be there.** Working the field. Doing the right thing and trying your best. If you do not get the play it is because the best quarterback in the universe did not believe that at that time, you were in the right place doing the right moves. But as you learn how to pray, your game improves and every time you call, you will receive on time.

As we have mentioned before, it is not an act of toiling, like an ox passively pulling a plough down a long field. Unfortunately, this is what most humans do at work during their eight hours. The act of simply doing the least and getting through the day to collect a small wage is just another form of self-enslavement. The reason that the wages of a person that does the work are much lower than those of the person that thinks out the work is because the laborer lacks devotion; so he becomes expendable.

It is hard to petition The Lord for greater prosperity when you are tied down to the same wearisome routine.

Devotion is your challenge to accomplish things that are worthwhile. When you become devoted to something or someone, it is because your cycle is already in action. At this point you will be confronted with a dangerous paradox. Your good sense of duty and discipline may be promoting or supporting a terrible cause. Sometimes a person is so devoted to a cause that he becomes blinded to any surrounding persons or consequences. A fascination with a person, an item or a cause can turn a sense of devotion into a dangerous obsession.

I believe that many German citizens became obsessed with Hitler, not because of his personality or intelligence but because they really wanted a better Germany. The economic and political suffering of the nation under the Weimar Republic made millions of German citizens believe in Hitler. The same is true with the terrorist events of September 11, 2001. Fundamentalist Islamic fanatics became devotedly convinced that the way to improve on their people's misery was by destroying western prosperity. They even used God's name to justify their stupidity. But God is not with them, for prosperity is God given. If you do not have prosperity it is because your cycles are poor. Prosperity cannot be taken away from the person that is carrying out good cycles. Thus, the resolve of the American people to avenge the terrorist action, destroy their organizations and protect its prosperity is a cause just as devoted. Both, the Germans and the Islamic terrorists never thought that their devotion could bring about their destruction.

Therefore, you must be careful of what you really want, because with devotion, you shall have it.

Your prayer will be answered and you may not like the details. You may find yourself like one of those people that dreamt and worked to become famous and once their prayers were answered they hated the stalking by fans and the paparazzi. This is why it is important to be specific in what you are praying for. Never confuse your objective.

A while back, when in college, I became friends with a young priest from Central America. At lunch in the cafeteria we would reminisce about the beauty of our tropical countries and the warmth of the lifestyle. But my new friend had a fervent political mind that believed in socialist revolution as the only way to eradicate corruption, tyranny and social injustice.

He believed that the communist guerrillas were the heroes and he would express his revolutionary ideas vociferously to anyone that would hear. He was passionate, obsessed and frustrated.

Although he was an atheist, he had started a cycle with his thoughts and with his words. It was a **prayer by omission.** His frustration made him take the third ACTION step. Motivated by rage, and left the school, traveling to the mountains of Nicaragua and joining the Sandinista guerrillas. He was devoted to the cause of bringing down the Somoza dictatorship.

Six months later, I was saddened to hear that he had died in some unimportant firefight.

He had always expressed a desire for justice for his people, and with this "excuse" he had gone to war - "to fight for peace" - which was the total oxymoron of his objective. Instead, what he had started in rage was a cycle that would lead him to his immediate objective, which was a life of violence. Without ever thinking of his unfortunate outcome, he had quit an academic life to join an organization whose business was fighting violent battles on a daily basis.

What then, could he hope for?

He could have fought his battle from an academic or a spiritual standpoint. After all, being an intellectual was his strength. Instead, he went to join a fighting group without having the most minimal military knowledge. So, he had started a cycle with his thoughts and words and when the time came to act he found himself at a fork in the road.

Sure enough, as Americans we realize that peace and social justice required a fight, but with each person following a different set of cycles. He could have devoted himself to his cause within his area of knowledge. But instead he devoted himself to the cause impulsively. He took the wrong road when he betrayed what he knew best. He lost sight of the fact that the immediate expectation of war is everyone's destruction.

But his prayer had been answered. His cycle, which started with his rage, was completed with his destruction.

Be devoted to yourself first. Remind yourself of that instruction you receive from the flight crew when you board an airplane. *"Place the mask on yourself first before you help others including children or elderly"*. Because you must survive first in order to help anyone else.

The loss of devotion to one's self is the cause for poor health and the alienation of loved ones.

Although devotion is an egoist feeling, it is a source of enthusiasm and happiness and should not be confused with obsession or paranoia. Only the person that considers himself devoted to God and fanatically believes that his religion is the only true one, is in reality the obsessed.

Hence there is a difference between those who are devoted to God, and those "who feel" that they are devoted.

The devoted person (no matter who or what he may be devoted to) places his devotion to the test. He is not afraid to take the risk of finding out what is true. He really wants results. He starts a cycle towards an objective. He is centered to the point of egoism in his thoughts but shares his faith and his results with those participating with him. He is a prosperity seeker.

"Sometimes people don't want to hear the truth
Because they don't want their illusions
destroyed" - Friedrich Nietzsche

The person, "who thinks" he is devoted, will seek a leader to follow and follow his leader's ideas blindly. He will be obstinate and afraid of taking any risk for fear of finding that the truth is not in agreement with his beliefs. He only shares with those that surround him and whom he considers worthy of his attention. He never acts alone and he is a status seeker and worse of all, he compromises his religious beliefs to fit his political views.

Devotion to your objective is the easiest way to God. Believe in God and pray every day and a feeling of calm will permeate your mind for only the person that is truly devoted to his own purpose and his cause will obtain what he was expecting.

9

CHALLENGES AND HOW DOES IT AFFECT OUR PRAYERS
✛ ✛ ✛

Challenges and limitations

Interestingly, you can affect and modify various things along YOUR path. Things such as time, attitude, tolerance, sharing, giving, resources, and other factors, that will play an important role in the final outcome of your prayer.

Remember that the prayer shall be the start and completion of a Divine Cycle through actions or omissions. The following checklist will help to start a cycle correctly:

The prayer is the cycle of a thought, its words, actions, (work, attitude) and re-start. I suggest you write down your thoughts as though each were a project so that you may clarify them. When praying to The Lord, choose your words carefully. No matter how tough you are, avoid profanity in all your words. Make sure that you will act positively on those words. Convert those words into commitments. Do not bluff. A prayer is not a poker game. Do not pray in jest. The Lord may confuse your poor humor with cynicism. Do not pray in silence. **The Lord cannot hear your thoughts.**

The words of commitment will become actions in the direction that you want to go. Maintaining direction is your work. After completion, feel good about your accomplishment and polish your process.

Establish exactly what you will be praying for. Then look at yourself for one minute, and determine if your values match those of the society where you will be making your request. If they are not, then ask yourself? Can I change, or, can I make my community change?

Invoke God by calling His name and pronouncing The Lord's Prayer. Remember: This is the ONLY prayer taught to mankind by Jesus and it is extremely effective.

DO NOT QUIT. QUITTERS ARE NOT REWARDED.

Act with faith. Whatever you do not know, or whatever part is missing in your search for an answer will present itself, when you maintain devotion to the cycle.

Be devoted to your cause to your team and to your resources. Place confidence in your team and share your work, and your prosperity.

Start anew and repeat. The prayer must be constant and the process a continuous one. Regrouping is essential and it takes time, so do not desist. Even if you have an uphill battle, if the process is good and it is continuously refined and tuned, you will obtain good results.

"All human beings can alter their lives
by altering their attitudes" - Andrew Carnegie

When acting with faith, act with **good mood, courage and focus.** A good attitude will be necessary to transcend the challenges that will be encountered in our path.

Your determination shall be tested. God wants to know if you are really worthy of what you are praying for. Three types of challenges shall be placed before you. These challenges will come from three main sources: from **Nature,** from your own **Sins**, and from **God.** I call them the Natural Challenge, The Challenge of Sin and The Divine Challenge.

The power to crossover these obstacles will be proof to God that your prayer needs to be answered positively.

The Natural Challenge

Man is not created good or evil. Simply, evil appears as a creation of the conflicts to which humans are subjected daily. The stress to our bodies and our minds sometimes numbs the correct feelings that we should have for our fellow man. We are born into a life where we do not choose our family or geographical place of birth, and unfortunately this ancestry creates different natural, physical, and economic conditions for all of us.

This is the natural challenge: **To adapt yourself with the deck of cards that life has dealt you since birth.**

Having only this life to live, we must realize that the natural challenge is only a part of the game of life. In the natural challenge, there is no reward or penalty for being a good or bad person. Evidence has shown that the good people do not move any faster through rush hour traffic. Or that the weather is nicer for good people than for regular sinners.

Adaptation here is the key. Natural challenges cannot be changed very much with prayer. No matter how much you may plead to the Lord, if you leave your downtown workplace at 5:00

p.m. you will be stuck in rush hour traffic. If you decide to build your house in San Francisco, you will sooner or later have to experience an earthquake. If you live in a farm on a desert you will have to toil harder to make the land prosper. Surpassing the natural challenge requires more effort than prayer.

When it comes to nature, the creation of our planet was made perfect to sustain life. This creation involves the planet having necessary earthquakes and hurricanes and tornadoes and all sorts of natural violent activity. It's the way our planet lives and makes an environment possible for humans and others to live. We cannot complain if human suffering is caused by these events because these events is what makes life possible.

Sometimes we interpret great natural disasters such as earthquakes, floods or hurricanes as a punishment from God. But in reality these are actions designed billions of years ago to maintain the process of creation functioning in a perfect order. A great hurricane is sometimes what The Earth needs to cool an overheated section of the atmosphere.

Human beings in an act of necessity, ignorance or arrogance simply decide to ignore science and build in the path of hurricanes, in flood plains or in earthquake zones. When disaster strikes, we search for answers to why God sent such "punishment". But where you live is a matter of personal choice and it involves no-fault risk, therefore, God cannot be blamed for natural occurrences.

But no matter where you have been born, or where you live the conditions and resources will exist to make life good. You can prepare yourself for the unanticipated and take measure of the geographical risk. When building in California it is more effective to improve construction techniques, than to ignore the building codes and then pray to God for protection.

Therefore, the natural challenge is the product of humans coping with creation. Nature is very difficult to alter, but it teaches us that in all circumstances and conditions, the same human virtues apply, and through negotiation and cooperation we can successfully adapt to any environment.

There is no reason to fear the possibility of failure because you will be provided with the necessary elements to live well if you make the effort to adapt to the people and the elements that surrounds you.

Life is a gift and is meant to be good. Playing the game of life should not be one of suffering; because suffering in this life is no guarantee of a better after life. The challenge is to adapt yourself to the existing environment, and to choose and improve your playing field where your life can be joyful and productive.

The Challenge of Sin

The second challenge is the challenge of sin, and it is the most complicated, because it defines our own existence. It compels us to ask: what kind of person am I?

Sin is not necessarily the "dark" or the "bad". We all realize that killing is "bad", but as Americans we know that we obtained our freedom by fighting in wars where many killings occurred. Those who fought in those wars are not remembered as bad people but as the heroes that preserved the existence of our nation.

As Sergeant York demonstrated in The World War of 1914, something as "bad" as killing, may become a necessity that has a rewarded result. Sometimes a soldier carries out God's work better than a priest does.

The Bible is full of battle orders that were carried out to guarantee the survival of the people of Israel.

"Sleep does not help, if it's your soul that is tired" - Michelle Brookhous

So, how do we know what action is really bad, as opposed to doing something "bad" that could have a positive result.

Deciphering this dilemma is the challenge of sin. The truest definition of Sin is: **Causing damage to our own selves or causing damage to others.**

And it becomes worse when you ignore common wisdom and cause this damage deliberately.

Sin enters our life because the universe was created on the concept of duality and parallel contradictions. So, from the minute a person says: "I can do this." Someone will say: "No you can't." And if you say something should be light, someone will come out and say it should be dark. There will always be an opposition. No matter whether your project is good or bad or if it has merit or not, in this game of life there will always be someone blocking your way.

Any football player knows that an opposing player immediately upon the start of the play will tackle him. The challenge is to surpass your blocker. This situation can obviously become quite stressful and our impulses sometimes order us to proceed violently against this tackle. But the challenge of sin is to play the game cleverly without destructive harm.

A sin is a cry of "FOUL" in the game of life. It is the violation of your right or of someone's right to pursue happiness and prosperity. It is the temporary or permanent negation of a fair play in the game of life where there IS ALWAYS adversity. There is nothing wrong being a good player or trying to be the best. It may cause jealousy or envy, but there is a reward when the game was played clean. But it is a sin when you play rough, knowing that someone, including yourself can get seriously hurt.

When you sin in the game of life, you are immediately punished by the referee, or distanced by the rest of the players. The payback, also known as karma, is not in a future after life; it is in THIS life.

Unfortunately, many people feel that the penalty for sinning will be in a future place called hell, which may or may not exist after death occurs. As a result they continue a negative behavior in this life that eventually makes THIS present life hell for themselves and for those who love them.

The penalty is paid during this life.

Sin produces loneliness. Sometimes you sin with someone or against someone and you find yourself losing a friend, hiding from someone or even in prison. Sometimes the sin is against our own selves. Like when we are having a drug or food addiction and as a result we alienate people.

This concept of duality and parallel contradictions, establishes that, for everything that acts, something else will react, no party can act alone to obtain a material result without another opposing it. Someone must give and someone must receive. Every dark side has a bright side. Nothing is entirely good without having something bad.

Both, your actions and omissions, therefore, can make you sin. Sinning because you caused a negative action is easy to comprehend. It is a sin to steal from someone.

But mediocrity or weakness causes sinning by omission. In this case, you sin because you allowed yourself to become the consequence of someone else's premeditated bad action; you become guilty of conspiracy. This is why the law considers the accomplice just as guilty as the criminal who actually committed the act. Both sinned, even if one of them did not like what the other did.

Confront upfront those who tempt you before small pains become great sorrows.

Confronting the situation or the person you are praying about is essential to accomplish your prayer. When not confronted, very small mistakes become great tragedies. A small problem is like a small leak in a dam. It must be addressed with urgency, usually bearing a small cost. Left unattended it becomes a disaster.

There is no art in war but there is in confrontation. Especially when confrontation must be peaceful to avoid sinning. It requires tact, character, strength, knowledge and determination. Learning to confront builds courage and the challenge of sin is surpassed with courage. The requirement in the amount of courage is much less at the beginning of a situation.

Every human being, regardless of upbringing, realizes the difference between right and wrong at a very early age. In subsequent years, greed, anger and other factors may blind him in making this differentiation. But deep down every being knows when it is right to say NO or YES to a situation. In this differentiation lies the ability to avoid sin with all its unhappy consequences.

The Divine Challenge

Any person that has read The Book of Job, probably realizes that the Will of God and its immensity cannot be totally understood at all times by the human mind.

We are confronted daily by climate, disease, temptation, and a multitude of factors that make us act and react in good and bad ways. The most important thing is to learn how to deal with each situation as it presents itself, in a way that does not sacrifice your wellness.

The Divine challenge is to improve our own selves by finding God. It is a duty to rise above ignorance and prejudice, and to learn the proper virtues that are needed to obtain happiness, health and financial security.

In the Divine challenge, the challenge is to search for the

truth on our own, and knowing that the truth is what works positively and not necessarily what is taught by religious dogma. To accomplish this, you must learn to forgive.

As we mentioned before, time is relative to the decay of our bodies. If we were to live forever, we would probably carry on with our petty differences and hatreds for millions of years. The spirit knows that God has set a time limit to life, and within that time we must strive to seek happiness and peace of mind by forgiving those with whom we have quarreled.

During the era of The Roman Empire, all great avenues would lead in and out of Rome. Well, it is the same in our search of God. There are many philosophical avenues, perhaps all valid. Each avenue cuts through a different terrain and it's the difficulty in dealing with the topography what sets humans apart.

Each group tries to predicate the right way to travel but they fail to realize that the road they have chosen has taken them through totally different places. Some roads are simply more arduous than others. Although each road will be different, the purpose of travel, and the destination is the same.

So, the Divine challenge is to maintain the focus on a positive process and sequence of praying cycles and in this way surpass all abysms. By doing this God will always provide.

APPENDIX

I want to make brief mention of those from whose wisdom I borrowed to write this book. The success of these masters is proof that prayers are answered when the correct protocols are followed.

Andy Andrews. *b.May 22,1959.Alabama. American Author, Corporate Speaker and Coach.*

Marcus Aurelius. *b. April 121. Roman Emperor. Prior Roman Consul adopted by Emperor Hadrian and designated as heir because of his wisdom. Philosopher. Author of The Meditations.*

Michelle Brookhaus. *American Author, Homeopath and Wellness Coach.*

Niels Bohr. *b.Oct.1885. Danish physicist. Nobel Prize in Physics 1922.*

Buddha. *b.563? BC. Nepal. Known as Siddhartha Gautama Buddha. "The Awaken". Sage, teacher, Founder of Buddhism.*

James Cameron*. b. Aug. 1954. Canada. Movie producer and Director. Winner of The Oscar for Best film 'Titanic'. National Geographic Explorer.*

Julius Caesar. *b. 100 BC. Roman Consul, General and Emperor. Last name* *adopted as title for 'Supreme King' by other cultures such as Kaiser and Tsar.*

Andrew Carnegie. *b.Nov.1835. Scotland. Naturalized American who founded Carnegie Steel (became United States Steel), business magnate, philanthropist.*

Betty Eadie. *b.1942.Nebraska. American Author of several books on Near Death Experiences.*

Tomas A. Edison. *b.Feb 1847. Ohio. American inventor best known for the incandescent light bulb. Established the Menlo Park Labs. Awarded many patents.*

Ralph Waldo Emerson. *b.May 1803. Massachusetts. American writer and philosopher who explored principles of self-reliance, nature, individuality and freedom.*

M.C.(Maurits Cornelis) Escher.*b. June 1898. Netherlands. Graphic artist known for bizarre optical and conceptual effects such as ladders that return to the same plane and hand that drafted themselves.*

Albert Einstein. *b. March 1879. Germany. Theoretical physicist who developed the theory of Relativity (E=mc2).Nobel Prize winner in Physics in 1921. Escaped Nazi Germany and became a Naturalized U.S. Citizen and professor at Princeton University.*

Epictetus. *b.55. Greece. Stoic Philosopher of the 1ˢᵗ century. Born into slavery to a secretary of Emperor Nero. Freed after the Emperor's death, Epictetus became a writer and teacher of ethics, logic and self-knowledge.*

Nassim Haramein. *b.1962. Switzerland. Physicist known for exploring a unified field theory that brings together the physical and metaphysical worlds. Founding member of The Resonance Science Foundation.*

Stephen Hawking. *b.Jan 1942. England. Physicist and Cosmologist. Expert* *in General relativity and Quantum Mechanics. Author of many best sellers. Professor at Cambridge University.*

Oliver Wendell Holmes Jr. *b. March 1841. Massachusetts. American Jurist and Chief Justice of The Supreme Court in 1902.*

William James. *b. January 1842. New York. American philosopher and psychologist. First educator to offer a psychology course in The U.S.*

John F. Kennedy. *b. May 1917. Massachusetts. Democrat Senator. 35ᵗʰ President of The U.S.*

Dalai Lama. (14ᵗʰ) *b. 1935. China. Spiritual Leader of the Tibetian people. Teacher of Buddhism. The 14ᵗʰ Dalai Lama received the Nobel Peace prize in 1989.*

John, Writer of the 4ᵗʰ Gospel. *Most likely the Gospel of John has an anonymous writer and credits John The Apostle.*

John Lennon. *b. October 1940. England. Singer, songwriter, poet and founding member of The Beatles.*

Benoit B. Mandelbrot. *b. Nov. 1924. Poland. Mathematician recognized for study in fractal geometry.*

Margaret Mead. *b.December 1901. American anthropologist. Author of 'Coming of Age in Samoa'.*

Joyce Meyer. *b.June 1943. Missouri. Charismatic Christian author and speaker. Founder of Joyce Meyer Ministries.*

Mike Murdock. *b.April 1946. Louisiana. American Pastor, songwriter, televangelist. Founder of The Wisdom Center Ministry. Known for his promotion of prosperity theology.*

Friedrich Nietzche. *b.Oct 1844. Germany. Philosopher whose work on* *existensialism, cultural criticism, nihilism and fact-value distinction paved the way for 20ᵗʰ century thinking.*

Joel Osteen. *b. March 1963. Texas. Non-denominational Christian Televangelist. Pastor of Lakewood church. Founder of Joel Osteen Ministries.*

George Orwell. *(pen name of Eric A. Blair) b. June 1903. England. Novelist whose works reflected cultural behavior and social injustice.*

Carl Sagan. *b. Nov. 1934. New York. American Astronomer and astrobiologist. Professor at Cornell University. NASA distinguished Public Service Medal.*

George Bernard Shaw. *b. July 1856. Ireland. British playwriter and political activist. Nobel Prize in Literature 1925.*

Will Smith. *b. Sept. 1968. Pennsylvania. American actor and comedian.*

Seneca. *b. 4 BC. Spain (then a Roman province). Roman stoic philosopher and statesman. Advisor to Emperor Nero (under duress).*

Charles M. Schwab. *b. Pennsylvania 1862. American Industrialist. Bethlehem Shipbuilding & Steel. business magnate. (No relation to Charles Schwab brokerage).*

Lao Tzu.(aka Laozi) *b. 500BC?. China. Ancient philosopher credited with founding Taoism/Daoism.*

Oprah Winfrey. *b. Jan 1954. Mississippi. American Journalist, actress and media magnate. Founder of various media/communication enterprises and shows.*

Upanishads. *800 BC. A series of Hindu sacred treatises expounding the Vedas -the oldest scriptures of Hinduism, 1500 BC? - in mystical terms.*

Zen. *618. China. School of Buddhism strongly influenced by Taoism. Focus on insight as a path to enlightenment. Zen also derives knowledge from the ancient Vedas and incorporates Yoga —a spiritual physical discipline-in its practice.*

Printed in the United States
By Bookmasters